GORAN OHLIN

FOREIGN AID POLICIES RECONSIDERED

DEVELOPMENT CENTRE
OF THE ORGANISATION
FOR ECONOMIC CO-OPERATION AND DEVELOPMENT

The Organisation for Economic Co-operation and Development was set up under a Convention signed in Paris on 14th December 1960 by the Member countries of the Organisation for European Economic Co-operation and by Canada and the United States. This Convention provides that the OECD shall promote policies designed :

— *to achieve the highest sustainable economic growth and employment and a rising standard of living in Member countries, while maintaining financial stability and thus to contribute to the development of the world economy ;*
— *to contribute to sound economic expansion in Member as well as non-member countries in the process of economic development ;*
— *to contribute to the expansion of world trade on a multilateral, non-discriminatory basis in accordance with international obligations.*

The legal personality possessed by the Organisation for European Economic Co-operation continues in the OECD, which came into being on 30th September 1961.

The Members of OECD are : Austria, Belgium, Canada, Denmark, France, the Federal Republic of Germany, Greece, Iceland, Ireland, Italy, Japan, Luxembourg, the Netherlands, Norway, Portugal, Spain, Sweden ,Switzerland, Turkey, the United Kingdom and the United States.

CONTENTS

Preface *by Robert Buron* 7

I. Introduction 9
II. The Evolution of Aid Doctrine 13
III. Public Opinion on Foreign Aid 55
IV. The Volume of Aid and its Measurement 65
V. Forms of Financial Aid 85
VI. Towards a Code of Development Assistance? 99

Annex

The grant element in development lending, and the growth of service charges 101

Bibliography 113

⁂

List of Tables

I.1. Official Bilateral Assistance to Developing Countries from DAC Member Countries, 1960-1963 10
IV.1. The Flow of Official Financial Resources from Industrial OECD Countries to Developing Countries and Multilateral Agencies, 1950-1963 (Disbursements) 66
IV.2. Interest Rate and Length of Maturity, 1961-1963. Official Bilateral Loan Commitments by Industrial OECD Member Countries Combined 67
IV.3. An Approximate Balance of Payments for OECD Countries with Less Developed Countries, 1962 68
IV.4. Discounted Value of Official Bilateral Gross Loans from OECD Member Countries 73
IV.5. Net Flow of Official Ressources to LDC's and Estimated Real Cost of Commitments, 1963 75
IV.6. Shares of Ten Donor Countries by Various Methods of Assessment 76
IV.7. Summary of Estimates of the Savings Gap 77
IV.8. Summary of Estimates of the Foreign Exchange Gap 79
IV.9. Geographic Distribution of Official Bilateral Grants from OECD Member Countries to Developing Countries, 1962 81
IV.10. Geographic Distribution of Official Bilateral Net Lending from OECD Member Countries to Developing Countries, 1962 82
IV.11. Per Capita Official Bilateral Grants from OECD Member Countries, 1962 .. 82
IV.12. Per Capita Official Bilateral Lending from OECD Member Countries, 1962 .. 83

IV.13.	Per Capita Assistance to Developing Countries per Region from OECD Member Countries, 1962	83
IV.14.	Net Official Capital Flow from OECD Countries and Multilateral Agencies Combined in 1962 and Capital Aid Requirements According to Rosenstein-Rodan	84

Annex

1.	Grant Element in Loans of 10 Years Maturity	111
2.	Grant Element in Loans of 20 Years Maturity	111
3.	Grant Element in Loans of 30 Years Maturity	112
4.	Grant Element in Loans of 40 Years Maturity	112

PREFACE

The Organisation for Economic Co-operation and Development has as one of its principal tasks the confrontation of member countries in regard to various aspects of their economic policies. One of these aspects concerns the effort to assist the development of less developed countries, in which most Western nations are engaged. It was, therefore, normal that the Development Centre of the OECD should attempt to analyze the character and evolution of these aid policies in recent years.

No one could have been better chosen than Professor Goran Ohlin for this delicate task. As a historian, Professor Ohlin has throughout his study emphasized how the notion of aid has developed — first conceived by governments as an inescapable element of their foreign policy, but increasingly seen as an effort to guarantee the peace and prevent the spread of disorder in the *tiers monde,* and recognized by the common man as an expression of human solidarity between the poor and the deprived, in spite of a *cartierist* or isolationist opposition which hopes to have a good conscience cheaply.

Although international solidarity is gaining substance and although a certain quantitative improvement has taken place in the developing countries, the gap between the rich and poor countries has not ceased to increase. The expansive force of the industrialized countries with their immense technological capacity is such that it is almost impossible to imagine any catching up in present conditions, even if a very considerable joint effort is invested in it. In the opinion of many, the best one can hope for is the maintenance of the present disequilibrium situation.

*
* *

Professor Ohlin's study contributes to our knowledge of the motives behind the aid policies in the developed countries, and to the evaluation of their results. Moreover, it seems to me to lead to three basic propositions which I, as President of the Development Centre, should like to make with address both to the leaders of the developing countries and to economic policy makers in the advanced industrialized countries.

1. The problem of development, which affects two-thirds of humanity, will not be solved quickly. It is a long run matter. In order to be effective, development assistance, whether financial or technical, must have an impact both on material infrastructure and on the psychological conditions which ultimately determine the outcome. Such efforts require much time before they bear fruit.

2. But the problem of development assistance is indivisible and must be approached as a whole. It is necessary to provide underdeveloped coun-

tries both with funds and with technical know-how; the multiplication of uncoordinated approaches and the consequent wastage must be avoided.

3. In spite of the difficulties stemming from what governments consider their legitimate interests — to put it briefly, the national egotism of the donors, and also of the recipients — co-ordination of aid policies is possible and necessarily increases their efficiency. On the donor side, the persistent labours of the Development Assistance Committee of the OECD are leading to valuable results. The practice of mutual confrontation of aid policies has been accepted by donor countries, and an important breakthrough has thus been made towards what one sometimes calls "the multilateralization of bilateral aid". This is the direction in which those responsible for development assistance policies should move, and gradually and slowly they are doing so.

The current moment is one of stocktaking and reappraisal everywhere. The necessity of an overhaul of the methods so far employed is accepted by all. Some progress is also being made towards the idea that it is not enough to co-ordinate the giving of aid, but that its utilization must also be multilateralized. To the extent that Mr. Ohlin's study might contribute to such and other conclusions, it will be especially useful.

I
INTRODUCTION

Whether foreign aid should be called a new phenomenon or not depends on one's point of view. In the history of diplomacy, subsidies and tributes have been common, and wartime aid among allies was already given by Britain during the eighteenth century and the Napoleonic wars, but peacetime economic aid among governments is novel[1]. It is true that English and French capital exports to underdeveloped regions just before the First World War exceeded the present flow of capital to underdeveloped countries, and that colonial government in many respects served the end of economic development. Generally speaking, the West has been involved in the economic development of the rest of the world since the time of the Discoveries.

Yet, the use of public funds for the specific purpose of promoting and assisting in the economic development of other sovereign countries has no significant precedent before the Marshall plan, and its present place as an element in the relations between advanced and underdeveloped parts of the world is first and foremost a consequence of the profound change in those relations after World War II.

Only fifteen years ago, development assistance was of marginal importance, but since then it has made enormous strides. To measure it adequately is a difficult task which will be discussed later, but by the standard international measurements the flow of public grants and loans for economic assistance increased by about 12.5 per cent per annum between 1950 and 1962. It currently runs at about 6 billion dollars a year, which is probably between one-third or one-quarter of the capital formation in the underdeveloped continents of the world, and corresponds to about one-fifth of their export earnings from industry.

More important still is the recognition of foreign aid as a distinct area of public policy in all advanced countries. New national and international agencies for its administration and co-ordination have emerged and a considerable body of experience has been accumulated, no less valuable for the fact that much has been frustrating. Problems of development policy, including aid policy, have received unprecedented attention on practical and theoretical levels. The dissatisfaction which still prevails with regard to the understanding of basic problems of economic development should not blind one to the fact that a new discipline of knowledge and a new profession of specialists are taking shape.

---

1. For the fanciful claim that subsidies and grants in antiquity should be regarded as a form of development aid, see Franz Altheim, *Entwicklungshilfe im Altertum* (1962).

Lately, the upward surge of foreign aid has shown signs of flagging. The budgetary funds committed for loans and grants of economic assistance have even fallen off, although disbursements continue to rise (Table I.1).

TABLE I.1. OFFICIAL BILATERAL ASSISTANCE TO DEVELOPING COUNTRIES FROM DAC MEMBER COUNTRIES, 1960-1963

Million US Dollars.

YEAR	COMMITMENTS	DISBURSEMENTS
1960	5,704	4,236
1961	6,774	5,205
1962	7,121	5,517
1963	6,764	5,912

NOTE. Only loans of maturities exceeding 5 years are included. For Belgium and France, no commitment figures are available, and disbursements have been used instead.

In some major donor countries, no further enlargement of the foreign aid programmes is likely in the immediate future. Frustration over political setbacks and instances of waste, and the realisation that, unlike the Marshall Plan, development assistance may become a very long-term undertaking have their part in the hesitance and stocktaking in donor countries. But there is also much confusion and uncertainty as to the basic rationale of aid policy. Eugene Black has remarked that foreign aid may be one of the areas "where governments develop a rationale for what they are doing only after having done it for quite a while first ».[1] The practice of foreign aid has many different roots, and the motives behind the foreign aid policy of one country may not be those that prevail in another.

The overwhelming part of development assistance is bilateral. Bilateral foreign aid policies are discussed with other donors and in some measure co-ordinated in the Development Assistance Committee of the OECD. The inclination is to regard them as part of a "common effort" on the part of advanced countries to assist the less developed ones. The volume and character of bilateral development assistance is extensively described in the OECD report on *The Flow of Financial Resources,* which also summarizes existing arrangements for the administration of aid in different countries[2]. What such descriptions reveal is how much bilateral aid policies differ in historical background, geographic orientation, and administrative tradition. Development assistance is a name covering many different relationships between suppliers and recipients[3].

When the "flows of assistance" from donor countries are compared, and when the global aspects of foreign aid are discussed, the emphasis tend to fall on aspects common to all aid policies rather than upon the circumstances and considerations unique to individual donor countries. But, in national

---

1. Eugene Black, *The Diplomacy of Economic Development* (1960), p. 54.
2. Latest edition : *The Flow of Financial Resources to Less-developed Countries. 1956-1963.* (Paris, 1964).
3. The semantics of foreign aid are of interest in themselves but not to the present study, and the suppliers of foreign aid will often, in accordance with current practice, be called « donors », even though their assistance may be in the form of loans. Nor is any attempt made to distinguish between "aid", "assistance" and "co-operation".

policy making, these singular factors loom large in the "philosophy" or "doctrine" on which aid is given. Much of the hesitation reflected in the retardation of growth in the overall volume of economic assistance and in domestic debates about foreign aid policies seems, in fact, to stem from a difficult reorientation from a historical to a new conception of assistance. To many donor countries, the primary policy question is not how much to devote to foreign aid. It is rather why and to whom foreign aid should be dispensed at all, for without an answer to such questions no clear philosophy of aid can be enunciated. Until now, much of the impetus behind foreign aid has been drawn from "special relationships", usually colonial links; in other cases, specific political and strategic objectives have been of great importance.

Neither the "advanced" countries nor the "underdeveloped" have by history been moulded into the bland stereotypes that these economic labels suggest and the ties that linked countries belonging to these two categories have been stronger than those than unite economic peers. But foreign aid derives from economic inequality and thus puts it plainly into focus. As the United Nations Conference on Trade and Development in Geneva in the Spring of 1964 demonstrated, economic backwardness is a sufficient cement for concerted action by the underdeveloped economies, at least in the statement of their views. The countries on the donor side also find themselves thrown together by their shared preoccupations with problems of assistance policy. This raises, to many of them, the essentially new problem of a policy towards the "underdeveloped countries" in general. One of the principal themes in the present reconsideration of foreign aid policies in donor countries is precisely that which is posed by a transition from a particular to a universal relationship to the *tiers monde*.

The purpose of this report is not to describe in detail the activities in the field of foreign aid, or to discuss the technical problems posed by development assistance, let alone to analyse the task of development planning in a broad sense. It is simply to make a preliminary enquiry into the tangled maze of motives and arguments behind the adoption of foreign aid policies in the industrially advanced countries. The emphasis will be on national policies, and the policies and techniques of development assistance by international organisations will not be discussed.

In the course of 1963, three major documents on foreign aid policy appeared in the principal Western donor countries: the Clay Report in the United States, the so-called Jeanneney Report on French foreign aid policies, and the British white paper called *Aid to Developing Countries*. These documents had one thing in common: they all attempted to clarify the role of foreign aid in public policy in their respective countries. It is true that they were different in scope, in style and function. Only one — the British white paper — was an authoritative policy statement. The others consisted of assessments and recommendations by private citizens summoned by their governments to consider an issue of great urgency. No one document could by itself reveal the range of positions and the degree of controversy or consensus with regard to foreign aid — or any other public policy — in any one country. But as attempts on a high level to reach an understanding of what foreign aid is and should be in the countries that furnish the bulk of world assistance, and as symptoms of a mood of reflection and a search for a rationale, these reports were of great interest and they sparked this study of the state of aid policy.

The following chapter will attempt to place them in the context of the changing outlook on aid in their countries, and it will also trace the emergence of specific foreign aid doctrines in other donor countries.

Substantial and recurrent claims on the public purse cannot, in democratic countries, do without a measure of public acceptance, and some of the difficulties of aid policy are assumed to stem from the hesitant attitudes of the public in industrial countries. Not very much is actually known about public opinion on foreign aid, but some evidence, such as it is, is presented in Chapter III. Chapter IV raises some of the problems connected with the measurement of development assistance and its distribution among donors and recipients, and Chapter V considers a few basic issues concerning the forms of financial assistance.

II

THE EVOLUTION OF AID DOCTRINE

It is impossible to escape the impression that one of the very real problems that plague Western foreign aid policies is a deep uncertainty and confusion about the nature and purpose of foreign aid. Such uncertainty affects the degree of political support that aid policies receive in donor countries, it obstructs co-operation and co-ordination among donors and strains relations between donors and recipients. The very language of foreign aid is far too often likely to simplify to the point of distortion, to mislead and to create false expectations in donor and receiving countries alike, with all the attendant hazards of disenchantment and rejection.

It is necessary to ask bluntly not only why advanced countries should give aid, but why, in fact, they do ? To be sure, there is a sense in which such a question is almost too complex to be answered: deliberations in councils of state are rarely disclosed, the considerations that sway the public are rarely known, and the relationship between public opinion and foreign and fiscal policy in general, let alone on this specific aspect, is extremely obscure.

It does not follow, however, that what is said and known about foreign aid polices is uninteresting or worthless. And what is said and known about such policies reveals very great difficulties in arriving at an understanding of what is one of the basic aspects of the relationship between the non-Communist industrialised countries and the "underdeveloped" countries. It is the nature of the relationship that is ultimately in question, and the present aspects of that relationship are so novel that the views and positions it evokes are not only various and conflicting, but frequently suffer from internal ambiguity and contradiction.

The purpose of emphasising the complexity of foreign aid policy is not to cast a slur upon the present foreign aid effort, but to contribute to the understanding of it. It is clearly a fact of momentous importance that development assistance in one form or another has become a virtually universal element in the relationship between advanced and industrial countries. There is a measure of significant consensus in the attempts to realise and understand why this has come to be. And that many different forces converge in the making of foreign aid policy is in the nature of political action. But confusion and uncertainty about what foreign aid is and should be is likely to be a weakness to any and all of its objectives.

Corresponding roughly to the distinction between multilateral and bilateral aid, there are currently two sets of doctrines about foreign aid for purposes of development assistance. (Although development aid is the principal subject of this essay, it is obvious that often no hard and fast distinction can be drawn between this and other types of assistance.) One is what might be referred to as the "international aid doctrine", the chief spokesmen for which have been international organisations and according to which the obligation of the advanced countries to assist the poorer ones simply follows from the demonstrated poverty of the latter. The second set of doctrines, vastly more complex, consists of arguments by which policies of economic aid are governed and justified in the countries that actually allocate public funds for development assistance, or undertake other activities under the heading of foreign aid.

THE UNITED NATIONS DOCTRINE

There can be no doubt that the principal vehicle of the conception that rich and advanced countries should assist poor and underdeveloped ones as a matter of moral principle and international solidarity has been the United Nations and the international agencies and organisations affiliated with it. The Charter speaks of the determination of the Members "to employ international machinery for the promotion of economic advancement of all peoples" and already in the first years of operations, much of the attention of the United Nations was directed towards problems of development aid. The preparation and publication by the United Nations of international statistics has brought home a world-wide awareness of the chasm between economic conditions in advanced countries and those in the large continents of Asia, Africa and Latin America, and laid the foundation for the claim that such inequality and such widespread deprivation within the international community establish a responsibility for rich nations, as well as a moral right to assistance on the part of poor ones.

The operations of the United Nations itself in the field of development assistance, and those of other international organisations, such as the IBRD, FAO, WHO, and UNESCO, rest on the effective strength of this sentiment. And in the language of international resolutions such as the U.N. General Assembly resolution of 1960 and the one recently accepted in Geneva at the UN Conference on Trade and Development, which urge upon advanced countries a contribution to development assistance of one per cent of their national income, no other principle is invoked than that of equity and human solidarity. This conception of international economic integration tends to imply a preference for assistance that is multilateral in the sense that it is administered by international organisations, and financed by assessments of the capacity to contribute on the part of the richer nations. It is also felt that aid should not be tied to procurements in he donor country, nor inspired by hopes of any returns, whether in the form of political or economic advantage of donors, Actually, as everybody knows, the reality is different. The bulk of development assistance — in 1963 as much as 84 per cent — is bilateral rather than multi-lateral, it is tied rather than untied, and it serves objectives far more complex than an international redistribution of income or of he scarce resources required for development.

This is not to say that the internationalist and humanitarian conception of foreign aid is without influence. It is, on the contrary, one of the strands woven into the justifications for foreign aid policies in all donor countries, and it will be argued later that it is indeed an effective force. But no small part of the confusion surrounding the subject of foreign aid results from the fact that this conception of why aid should be given is hopelessly inadequate as an explanation of why and how it is actually given. In domestic debates about aid policy in donor countries, moral and humanitarian viewpoints inevitably merge with more specific arguments purporting to show why a policy of granting foreign economic assistance is in the national interest. Nothing is gained by pretending to ignore that basic decisions regarding foreign assistance are made in a political context in which considerations of national interest must come to the fore.

It could not be assumed, however, that there is a clear consensus in individual donor countries as to the purpose and objectives of their foreign aid policies. In this, as in any other field, some degree of controversy is automatically engendered by the democratic process, but the novelty of the conception of foreign aid is such that even its basic raison-d'être is far from agreed upon.

THE UNITED STATES

Two-thirds of all development assistance emanates from the United States, where foreign aid programmes have been prominent ever since the end of the war. In the course of the shift from reconstruction in Europe to development assistance in the underdeveloped regions, the total amounts of foreign aid have declined very considerably, and in relation to GNP or Federal Budget expenditures the drop has been even greater. Thus, in 1949, economic assistance under the Marshall Plan amounted to about two per cent of GNP; at present official economic assistance amounts to one-third of one per cent of GNP. (Military assistance comes to another one-fourth of one per cent.)[1]

In spite of this relatively modest size and declining trend, the foreign assistance programme has never ceased to arouse unease and controversy. One of the manifestations of this has been the steady flow of special committees appointed to review this programme in depth. Since the inception of the Marshall Plan, there have been very few years in which foreign aid has not been the subject of reconsideration by some publicly appointed group of distinguished citizens.

Thanks to their reports and to the continuing dialogue between the Administration and Congress, the picture of United States aid doctrine is a good deal richer than in most other countries. The public debate on foreign aid has also been fuller in the United States than elsewhere. For this reason alone, it would be justified to give much space to the American search for an aid doctrine, as will, in fact, be done in this section. In addition, it might well be argued that the American debate has raised general issues with considerable relevance to other countries.

In the course of over a decade of argument, study, and administrative experimentation and growth, a US aid doctrine has, in fact, evolved with regard to objectives as well as techniques. Yet, it is possible, as sometimes claimed, that public confusion about the premises of United States foreign aid policy is waxing rather than waning. To the public and Congressional unease has recently been added sharp academic criticism and, so far from

---

1. *Proposed Mutual Defense and Development Programs, FY 1965*, p. 4.

being closed, the debate about first principles has been revived in the last years[1].

Technical assistance missions have been undertaken by the United States for more than a hundred years, especially in South and Central America[2], and the first major programme of economic assistance was, of course, the Marshall Plan. But it was not until 1949 that development assistance as such became national policy. The Point Four programme announced by President Truman in his inaugural address that year, and the subsequent act for International Development of 1950, made it "the policy of the United States to aid the efforts of the peoples of economically underdeveloped areas to develop their resources and improve their living conditions". In his inaugural address, the President described the "bold new program" as a task of "making the benefits of our scientific advances and industrial progress available for the improvement and growth of underdeveloped areas". He said explicitly that "the material resources which we can afford to use for the assistance of other peoples are limited. But our imponderable resources in technical knowledge are constantly growing and are inexhaustible".

This optimism about the catalytic effects of technical assistance also pervaded the presentation of the 1950 Act to Congress, but the spokesman for the Administration supplemented the appeal to humanitarianism and the President's call to action against "hunger, misery and despair" by relating development assistance both to the national economic interest of the United States itself and to the broad interests of United States security which had already warranted the massive economic and military assistance operations in Europe and more modest programmes in Asia. It was assumed that economic development could be promoted by U.S. technical assistance, and that it would contribute to political stability and resistance against Soviet penetration.

These objectives — charitable, economic, and strategic — have never been absent in considerations of U.S. aid programmes, and much of the debate about the basic purpose of a programme devoted to economic assistance — rather than military aid which raises fewer problems — has revolved around their interpretation and interrelationship. Whether economic assistance should be divorced, so far as possible, from diplomacy and from other forms of assistance, wether it should be bilateral or multilateral, whether it should be given widely or selectively, on more or less specific political terms — these questions have continued to confound aid policy, although in the end they have found more or less tentative answers.

After the inception of the Point Four programme, the Korean War turned the U.S. foreign aid effort in the direction of military assistance and defence support which claimed no other purpose than that of strengthening U.S. security, and for several years the problems of development assistance

---

1. See, e.g., Edward S. Mason, *Foreign Aid and Foreign Policy* (1964), and the essays collected in Robert A. Goldwin, ed., *Why Foreign Aid?* (1963).
2. The objectives of such missions are said to have been as mixed as those of modern aid programmes. They "grew out of a compound of economic interests, humanitarian sentiment, and strategic considerations. In most of these cases, the motives were so mixed that American aims were never clearly defined beyond a vague desire to maintain a series of reasonably stable republics". Merle Curti and Kendall Birr. *Prelude to Point Four* (1954), p. 205 ; cited in Charles Wolf, Jr., *Foreign Aid: Theory and Practice in Southern Asia* (1960), p. 13.

received little systematic attention, in spite of the growth of activities in that field. Technical assistance expenditures rose from 30 million dollars to 150 million a year, and a number of ad hoc programmes under the heading "assistance to economic development" found their way into the budget. The PL 480 sales of agricultural surpluses were started. But it was not until 1956-57, after a series of foreign policy set-backs and the appearance of the Soviet Union in the foreign aid field, that the United States foreign aid programme was suddenly subjected to the most intensive study and publicity it had yet received[1]. Reports were prepared by a Presidential Committee of Citizen Advisers, by the International Development Advisory Board appointed under the Point Four programme by the House Committee on Foreign Affairs, and by the Special Committee to Study the Foreign Aid Program set up by the Senate. The Special Committee contracted for eleven studies on different aspects of the foreign aid programme by private research organisations and also despatched ten individuals to survey foreign aid programmes in different parts of the world. According to the Chairman, Senator Green, the reason for this massive inquiry was the increasing opposition to the foreign aid programmes which seemed "to indicate either that their purposes have not been clearly understood, or that there is a growing belief that they have in some way failed to serve the national interest". The study[2], which filled over 1,500 pages, was intended to clarify the relationship between foreign aid and the national interest.

What emerged from these studies and reports was a range of positions and a definition of issues rather than a consensus, except possibly on the urgency of a policy vis-à-vis the newly independent states. The most forceful case for a distinctive and enlarged assistance programme, largely divorced from short-run foreign policy, though conceived to serve long-run interests of American security, was made in the report to the Senate Committee on "Objectives of the United States Economic Assistance Programs" by the MIT Center for International Studies, the ideas of which were also reflected in Millikan and Rostow's *A Proposal: Key to an Effective Foreign Policy*. The strategy of a major development aid programme proposed in this study rested on the proposition,

> that a comprehensive and sustained program of American economic assistance aimed at helping the free underdeveloped countries to create the conditions for self-sustaining economic growth can, in the short run, materially reduce the danger of conflict triggered by aggressive minor powers, and can, in say 2 to 3 decades, result in an overwhelming preponderance of societies with a successful record of solving their problems without resort to coercion or violence. The establishment of such a preponderance of stable, effective, and democratic societies gives the best promise of a favorable settlement of the cold war and of a peaceful, progressive environment[3].

This proposition in turn rested on the assumptions that assistance could stimulate growth, and that this could promote political maturity, not primarily

---

1. For a survey of this debate, see the papers by Schelling and Mason in *International Stability and Progress* (Eleventh American Assembly: New York, 1957).
2. U.S. Senate, Special Committee to Study the Foreign Aid Program, *Foreign Aid Program, Compilation of Studies and Surveys*, Washington, D.C., 1957, p. iii.
3. U.S. Senate, *Compilation*, p. 20.

by a rapid improvement in income, but by focussing nationalist energies, spurring meaningful action and supporting new and modernising elements in underdeveloped countries. Development aid should, it was suggested, be politically neutral:

> The United States agency allocating development funds should not have to consider anything beyond the technical criteria which have been established. It should never seek, for example, to influence negotiations on an airbase by granting or denying funds for construction of a hydro-electric station out of economic development appropriations[1].

Aid should be allocated so as to maximize additional effort, and two indices were suggested to measure such effort: steps to raise the marginal savings rate and capture increases in income for capital formation and the progress made in working out a development programme to enlarge the capacity to absorb additional capital productively. It was also suggested, however, that "capital aid should be offered wherever there is reasonable assurance that it will be effectively used ... Absorptive capacity becomes thus the measure of allocation of aid between different countries"[2]. Absorptive capacity was thought to be so limited,

> that relatively small amounts of capital ($2.5 to $3.5 billion more per year from all sources) would amply suffice even if every under-developed country of the free world were to avail itself fully of this opportunity. In practice, it is unlikely that more than 50 to 60 per cent of this amount would be taken up[3].

These features of the MIT and Millikan-Rostow proposals have been recalled because in many respects U.S. assistance policy has gradually incorporated many of them. Neither in 1957 nor later have they stood unopposed. At the opposite extreme, well-known economists argued that aid programmes "will almost surely retard economic development"[4], and political scientists that foreign aid programmes could not influence the course of political developments in Asia[5].

Closer to the main stream of the argument was the position of those who felt that development assistance inevitably was part of foreign policy, that the actual administration of such a programme neither could nor should be entirely separated from current diplomacy, and that the programme should be selective and generally serve to produce satisfactory political settlements[6].

In spite of such important differences about the precise relationship between aid policy and diplomacy, there was among those who recognized the need for economic assistance general agreement that the most important motive for such a policy was the concern with present and future political

---

1. *Ibid.*, p. 32.
2. *Ibid.*, p. 60-61.
3. *Ibid.*, p. 61. The study by the Research Center in Economic Development and Cultural Change at the University of Chicago also assumed that $3 billion was the additional need, rising to perhaps $5 billion in 10 or 15 years and then declining. *Ibid.*, p. 236.
4. Milton Friedman, "Foreign Economic Aid: Means and Objectives", *The Yale Review*, Summer, 1958. See also, e.g., the study prepared for the Senate Special Committee by the American Enterprise Association, Inc.
5. Z. Brzezinski, "The Politics of Underdevelopment", *World Politics*, October, 1956.
6. See, e.g., Mason, in the paper cited above.

developments in the world. The role and uses of the aid programme were variously interpreted, hopes and assumptions about the relationship between aid, development, political stability, and world peace were rarely spelled out, but it was recognized that, in the end, an aid programme must serve the interests of American national security in a broad sense. Probably nothing has caused greater misunderstanding than this proposition which could be taken to mean anything from the demand that American national policy should serve and not harm United States national interests to the suggestion that the aid programme should be dominated by the strategic exigencies of the cold war, and the furtherance of U.S. influence. Gunnar Myrdal wrote of a "strange suspicion on the part of the American people of their own generous motives" and called it a "slightly perverted element of their Puritan tradition"[1].

The aid-giving relationship was widely recognized as delicate, and the fear of seeming to exact political quid pro quos and instead incurring resentment or even refusals to accept economic aid led to positions such as Millikan and Rostow's, that "a program adopted for the wrong reasons may well be worse than useless". But, whether it was seen as an instrument of short-run influence, or as a bold investment in the future physiognomy of the world scene, the cases for the extension of economic aid took their departure in American interest rather than in that of the receiving countries — although the two were not supposed to be in conflict.

"Economic" cases for the promotion of economic growth in underdeveloped areas were occasionally cited in the 1957 debate. Then, as later, it was not infrequently asserted that the United States cannot indefinitely prosper in a world of poverty, that the development of export markets would be necessary to sustain employment and/or growth in the American economy, or that access to strategic raw material supplies in the underdeveloped regions could be a vital objective of development assistance. Such arguments are difficult to uphold, and few serious students maintained that economic gain in the narrow sense was, could, or should be an objective of economic assistance. Measures taken to stimulate private investment in underdeveloped countries were regarded favourably, especially as a means of transferring technology and skills, but it was never suggested that the promotion of U.S. investment could constitute an objective of assistance policy[2].

The role of the humanitarian and disinterested desire to assist the poorer countries has aroused heated controversy when held up as an alternative rather than a complement to the security objective. In 1957, as before and after, the generosity and philanthropy of Americans and the moral call to help were mentioned among motives for aid. It is clear that some part of postwar American aid, notably that consisting in private and volunteer action, has had this humanitarian character, it is probable that its importance to the public has been another than to makers of national policy, and it is

---

1. *An International Economy* (New York, 1956), p. 122.
2. A possible exception was the study for the Special Senate Committee on "American private enterprise, foreign economic development, and the aid programs", by the American Enterprise Association, Inc., which made no reference to the political objectives of aid programmes and was profoundly sceptical of the benefits of public aid. But even this report was said to aim at showing "how best to attain our main economic-based security objectives while minimizing the tax burden on Americans". U.S. Senate, *Compilations*, p. 545.

certainly possible that such motives have attracted individuals to foreign aid work. But it is unlikely that a simple desire to help has been an effective objective of United States aid policy in the sense that it has affected major decisions. As Charles Wolf, Jr., concluded in his survey of aid policy vis-à-vis South Asia, "in terms of this test, humanitarian objectives are not, nor do they appear likely to be, prominent among the continuing objectives of U.S. foreign aid"[1]. In Mason's view, "an aid program of some magnitude would be supported on relatively disinterested grounds", but by and large it would be misleading to assume that any sizeable part of United States economic assistance — or that from other countries — has flowed from such motives[2].

After the stocktaking in 1956 and 1957, the Senate and the House Committees recommended enlarged capital assistance in the form of loans on lenient terms, and with the creation of the Development Loan Fund in 1958 the shift towards development assistance was accelerated. The subsequent reorganisation — the establishment of A.I.D. — and the elaboration of U.S. aid philosophy in recent years, may be said to represent a crystallization around some of the positions emerging in 1957.

The foreign aid programme remained a topic of both controversy and consensus. Suspicions of waste and inefficiency were frequently expressed. The growing concern with the U.S. balance of payments made the foreign aid programme vulnerable to attack, and in the 1960's it excited more attention than ever[3]. In President Kennedy's foreign aid message of 1961, it was found necessary to "draw back and ask with candor a fundamental question : Is a foreign aid program really necessary ?"

In answer to this question, it was again asserted that "widespread poverty and chaos lead to a collapse of existing political and social structures" which would endanger the nation's security. The need for long-range planning and commitments was stressed, but the objective of development assistance was given special urgency by the suggestion that many of the less developed nations stood on the threshold of a break-through :

> The 1960's can be — and must be — the crucial "decade of development" — the period in which an enlarged community of free, stable, and self-reliant nations can reduce world tensions and insecurity[4].

In its largest sense, the objective of the foreign aid policy was described as that of creating a partnership between the northern and southern halves of the world, in which other industrialised nations would participate in a common effort. The need for internal reform and self-help in underdeveloped countries was again stated, but with special force in the formulation of a "new working concept" for the aid policy which distinguished between different types of

---

1. *Foreign Aid: Theory and Practice in Southern Asia* (1960), p. 284.
2. Mason, *Foreign Aid and Foreign Policy* (1964), p. 30.
3. A content analysis of successive State of the Union messages reveals that the percentage devoted to the foreign aid programme was :

Eisenhower:	1955	2 %	Eisenhower:	1958	2 %
	1956	3.5 %		1959	2.2 %
	1957	3.1 %		1960	6 %
			Kennedy:	1962	7.7 %

Cf. Jean Baptiste Duroselle et Jean Meyriat (eds.), *Politiques nationales envers les jeunes états* (Paris, 1964), p. 68.

4. H. Doc. 117, 87th Cong., 1st Sess. *Foreign Aid*. Message of the President to the Congress.

aid and development programmes proper to the recipients' stage of development and indicated that aid would be contingent on efforts of resource mobilisation, self-help, and internal reform.

The latest in the series of public committee reports on U.S. foreign aid is the Clay Report of 1963. The Committee submitting it was appointed by the President and had as its chairman General Lucius D. Clay. Its terms of reference were specific and in themselves express a characteristic of United States aid philosophy: the Committee was to examine U.S. military and economic assistance programmes to determine whether their scope and distribution was effectively contributing tot he security of the United States and the economic and political stability in the free world[1].

It was a brief and terse report. It recognised thet the foreign aid programmes served United States interests. Their "basic purpose" was said to be indicated by the high concentration of total foreign assistance to allies and other countries on the Sino-Soviet border which received 72 per cent of total (military and economic) assistance appropriations. The Committee criticised the dispersion of aid to an excessive number of countries. Specifically, it recommended that United States assistance to African countries should be limited to a minimum in view of European responsibilities there; claimed that economic assistance to some non-allied countries in Asia was "beyond that necessary for our interests"; and found the U.S. technical assistance programme too large to be adequately staffed with qualified personnel. The Committee was emphatic on the need for other industrialised countries to increase their aid effort, but believed immediate reductions to be in order in United States programmes, as it was "convinced that the burden of sustaining foreign assistance to the less-developed countries is falling unfairly upon the U.S." (p. 14). It especially urged the improvement of lending terms by other donors; otherwise "international consortia and co-ordinating groups for such countries as India, Pakistan, Turkey and Nigeria will saddle these countries with impossible debt-service requirements and U.S. funds would pay for these short-term and short-sighted debts" (p. 15).

In the long run, the Committee anticipated further reductions of U.S. assistance programmes and expected that repayment of old assistance loans would accelerate and provide an increasing share of the necessary funds.

The Committee favoured a gradual shift towards multilateral administration of aid which would insulate development assistance from political and commercial interests, be less susceptible to charges of infringing upon the sovereignty of recipients, and more co-ordinated than aid by many independent donors. It especially recommended the use of the International Development Association by the U.S. and its partners "as a common channel for aid funds, which would achieve many of our common objectives — a fairer sharing of the burden and the effective and coordinated use of the assistance provided on terms both appropriate to the needs of the recipient countries and impartial as among the commercial interests of the countributing nations" (p. 16).

On many traditionally controversial aspects of aid policy, the Committee also took restrictive positions: aid should not be given to establish "govern-

---

1. *The Scope and Distribution of United States Military and Economic Assistance Programs.* Report to the President of the United States from the Committee to Strengthen the Security of the Free World. Department of State, Washington, D.C., 1963.

ment-owned industrial and commercial enterprises which compete with existing private endeavours"; local costs of development projects should not be financed out of external assistance; terms of United States development loans should be harder where debt-servicing capacity was adequate.

The Committee did find the aid programme essential to United States security and noted that the need for development assistance was not merely a function of the cold war. Its tone was one of reluctant approval of a policy basically undesirable and exceptional, a regrettable but transient necessity, and in these respects, it reflected (and in some measure nurtured) the scruples and concerns about U.S. foreign aid policy which made the later Congressional struggle in 1963 one of unprecedented bitterness.

Nevertheless, the Clay report may be described as a brief and qualified endorsement of a policy which over the years has been restated and reviewed repeatedly. In recent years, this policy has been articulated into an AID doctrine which represents a remarkable advance towards the formulation of a systematic aid philosophy. The major objective of U.S. foreign assistance is now tersely described as that of assisting "other countries that seek to maintain their independence and develop into self-supporting nations"[1], as this offers the best long-run prospect of security and peace for the United States.

To use funds available for development aid as effectively as possible, "self-help is... the dominant theme" and the first criterion in allocating aid is said to be the effectiveness with which the recipient uses its available resources.

Countries in early stages of development are assumed to have a primary need for technical assistance and institution building, and only limited need for capital assistance, chiefly for infrastructure projects. As the need for capital assistance increases, the need for technical assistance shifts from general to more specific skills. The gradual increase in domestic savings, and a growing capacity to attract private and other conventional foreign capital on non-concessionary terms will progressively reduce the need for foreign aid. The assumption that the need for aid is temporary and limited is underlined — several recipients in Latin America and elsewhere are expected to attain rapid development in ten to fifteen years, but it is recognised that, in Asia and Africa, the need for aid will remain for a much longer time.

The sharpening definition of the objectives is also expressed in the concentration of funds. In the aid programme for fiscal year 1964-65, two per cent of assistance funds were destined to fourteen countries classified as "in transition toward self-support", ten per cent scattered over 37 countries for "limited programs" of different kinds, but 88 per cent concentrated on "major programs" in 25 countries. In this group, funds are further concentrated on seven countries — India, Pakistan, Turkey, Nigeria, Tunisia, Colombia and Chile — which are ranked highly in "self-help performance" and receive two-thirds of the U.S. development loans. The remaining 18 countries fall into two categories, one in which the "commitment to sound development policies and effective resource use" is found inadequate for programme assistance on a large scale and where aid takes the form of projects and technical assistance, and one in which problems of internal and external stability are overriding and

---

1. Agency for International Development, *Principles of Foreign Assistance*, Washington, D.C., 1963, p. 1,

where aid is furnished largely out of funds for "supporting assistance", rather than "development assistance"[1].

The official United States aid philosophy has thus reached a high degree of cogency and coherence compared with the early years of the aid programme. This is not to say that it has come to command the universal agreement even of serious students to foreign policy. In recent years, it has come under heavy fire from academic critics, attacking precisely the doctrine and rationale. Professor Hans Morgenthau contended that:

> of the seeming and real innovations which the modern age has introduced into the practice of foreign policy, none has proven more baffling to both understanding and action than foreign aid[2],

and claimed that the United States "has yet to develop an intelligible theory of foreign aid". In his view, development aid does not differ from the bribes traditionally employed in diplomacy, especially before the nineteenth century[3]. "The pretence and elaborate machinery" of development aid was said to result from a "climate of opinion" in which the obligation to assist underdeveloped nations and the possibility of promoting their development is accepted. "Economic development has become an ideology by which the transfer of money and services from one government to another in peace time is rationalised and justified" (p. 302). The possibility of promoting economic development in the underdeveloped countries was sweepingly denied on the grounds that preconditions for modernisation are lacking. Where ruling groups resist economic development, aid will fail in its ostensible purpose, strengthen the status quo, and accentuate social and political problems. Where aid is successful, the social disruption brought about by economic development will lead to political instability internally, and so far from promoting peace and external stability, it will increase the ability of more countries to wage war.

> The contrary conclusion derives from the popular, yet totally unfounded, assumption that "poor nations make war on "rich" nations for economic advantage and that "rich" nations are by definition peaceful because they have what they want (p. 307).

Professor Banfield, like Morgenthau, rejects the hopes placed on aid by reversing the proposition of the Millikan-Rostow chain of argument:

i) it is unlikely to make much difference to development which, where conditions allow, will come about without it, but in most countries will not;

ii) even if it does, it is unlikely to produce governments that are free, democratic, or even stable;

iii) peace is not promoted by economic development, let alons aid;

iv) even if the new states were to become entirely peaceful, this would not enhance the security of the United States[4].

---

1. *Proposed Mutual Defense and Development Programs, FY 1965.* Summary Presentation to Congress, Washington, 1964, pp. 22-23.
2. "A Political Theory of Foreign Aid", *The American Political Science Review*, June, 1962, p. 301.
3. See also George Liska, *The New Statecraft. Foreign Aid in American Foreign Policy* (1960).
4. Edward C. Banfield, *American Foreign Aid Doctrines* (1963); slightly different version in Goldwin, ed., *Why Foreign Aid?* (1903).

As for other benefits sometimes expected to flow from aid, they are described as equally illusory. The effect of aid upon opinion in receiving countries is as likely to be unfavourable as to be favourable, and the possibility of giving aid on a political quid pro quo basis is limited by the sensitivity of underdeveloped countries, but would otherwise be both morally and politically superior to the attempt to manipulate by the creation of diffuse obligations. Aid doctrine is thus said not to

> face up to the tragic facts which constitute the problem : that vast areas of the world will probably not achieve a very significant and widespread improvement in levels of living for at least several generations ; that they will probably not learn to govern themselves even tolerably well ; that such development as occurs is as likely to be inspired by hate as by good will or moral respect ; that it may, therefore, prove to be a disaster for the United States and for all mankind[1].

These sharp challenges of the case for development aid have been received as salutary antidotes to the clichés of aid discussion even by writers who find them fallacious and unwarranted[2]. In part, they rest on pessimistic assertions about social processes which are no more valid or demonstrable as generalisations than their opposites. In part, they rest on an appraisal of the realities of the underdeveloped regions and their importance which, it is contended, is inadequate. Above all, in their protest against the extravagant claims sometimes made for aid, they fail to appreciate the force of what might be termed the minimal case.

As Professor Millikan emphasised in his retort, virtually all recent crises of foreign policy have originated in the underdeveloped world, and the dangers for world peace and United States security that arise from political instability in the underdeveloped countries lie less in their potential hostility than in the involvement of the big powers and the escalation of bloc conflicts. Although indeed there are underdeveloped countries whose prospects of development are poor, there are several in which they are promising, and there is every reason to pursue a selective and discriminating policy of allocating aid to countries where it is productively used. In Professor Mason's view, the basis of a foreign aid programme can and should be "the demonstrated facts (1) that in at least a large part of the less developed world foreign aid can make and has made an effective contribution to economic development; and (2) that most countries, developed and underdeveloped, desperately want to be independent of external control"[3].

The American critics here cited contend that the process of modernisation is conducive to instability and that the prospects of economic growth are in many parts of the world dim and its consequences unpredictable. This is not denied in any quarter, but the real question, it is answered, is whether by a long-term aid policy "we can marginally influence the course of economic, social, and political modernisation so as to reduce somewhat the risks with which it confronts us"[4]. The House Committee on Foreign Affairs reached a

---

1. *Why Foreign Aid ?* p. 27.
2. Max F. Millikan, "The Political Case for Economic Development Aid", in Robert A. Goldwin, ed., *Why Foreign Aid ?* Edward S. Mason, *Foreign Aid and Foreign Policy*, Ch. 2, "Foreign Aid : In Search of a Rationale".
3. *Op. cit.*, p. 51.
4. Millikan, *op. cit.*, p. 107.

similar position in 1957 and its terse words sum up a case for aid echoed in many other aid-giving countries. It justified economic assistance on a number of grounds, but concluded :

> the most important reason is that nations are determined to develop. Only by participation in that process will we have an opportunity to direct their development along lines that will best serve our interests.

Even though one must take account of the United States' very special position among donor countries, the prolonged debate about U.S. aid is of interest for what it suggests about the intrinsic problems of reconciling foreign aid policy with democratic politics. It reveals a variety of motives for adopting a policy of economic aid to the developing countries, ranging from sheer charity to particular commercial or strategic interests. Much of the controversy has, in fact, concerned the motive rather than the policy, and some of the confusion which has attended the discussion of aid policy on this count has had it roots in simple misconceptions which haunt most aid debates.

In the first place, many arguments about the motives for aid flounder in the shifting sands on the border between conceptions of altruism and enlightened self-interest. The moral or even the political validity of aid is sometimes declared to be nil if there is even the slightest expectation of a benefit, whether in the form of gratitude, prestige, or influence ; and scattered voices among Western intellectuals in the former colonial powers have suggested that the colonial era of history has left a burden of guilt requiring some kind of expiation[1]. However, even the saintliest act is easily construed as self-interested, in a broad sense of the word, unless pathological or clearly self-destructive.

Secondly, public policy in a democratic society necessarily finds its support in a variety of motives and purposes. The task of generating effective agreement does not require that all must agree for the same reason. Foreign aid policies will be approached and interpreted differently, first of all by the various branches of government — departments of foreign affairs, finance, commerce, defence — and secondly by the electorate and its representatives to whom foreign aid policies, even when well understood, will necessarily mean many and different things and be approved or rejected for different reasons. In the United States, as elsewhere, the presentation of the foreign aid programme to the public has put relatively greater stress on the disinterested, humanitarian reasons to extend economic assistance than the deliberations in Congress. Yet, public opinion polls report a substantial majority in favour of foreign aid policies, which is sometimes contrasted with a more hesitant mood in Congress.

Thirdly, the issue of foreign aid tends to bring out sharply whatever doubts exist about the legitimacy or wisdom of pursuing — or appearing to pursue — national interests through diplomacy at all. What George Kennan terms "the legalistic-moralistic approach to international problems" comes to the fore in the uneasy feeling about the aid-relationship. It is strengthened by the internationalist emphasis on moral obligations and by the prickly sensitivity of receiving nations. Here the striving of aid-doctrine, in the United States and all other donor countries, has been to emphasise that, when economic progress is a shared objective, there is a community of interest

---

1. E.g. Arnold Toynbee, *The World and the West* (1953).

between donor and recipient, and to separate, wherever possible, development aid from current diplomacy and give it the character of long-run co-operation. Yet there is a persistent preoccupation, not only among recipient nations, with the issue of "strings" in the awarding of foreign aid, and with intervention in domestic affairs in the course of its implementation. Montgomery, in his study of U.S. aid policy, has even suggested that the doctrine of non-intervention has served to obscure the degree of involvement of the United States in other countries and weakened the diplomacy of foreign aid. "Repeated assertions of the non-political character of foreign aid have deceived Americans more than they have the leaders of the underdeveloped countries."[1] What in his view is lacking is "a rationale for the legitime and inevitable involvement that occurs in foreign aid relationships, and an understanding of both the opportunities and the limitations of such involvement"[2].

DECOLONISATION AND FOREIGN AID

What most sharply and fundamentally distinguishes the foreign aid policies of France and Britain, as well as of the lesser colonial powers, from that of the United States, is that, until recently, they have consisted almost entirely in a continuation of activities and policies of fairly long standing. This fact has determined not only the geographic distribution and the machinery, but also the motives and the character of the debate about policies which only with the coming of decolonisation have been referred to as "aid to underdeveloped countries".

This is not to say that colonial policy should be regarded as synonymous with development assistance. The general tenet of colonial administration was that public investment in colonies should be financed out of their own revenues. Government grants and loans for budgetary support or for projects specifically benefiting native populations remained exceptional until the interwar period. Private investment in overseas colonial territories was, of course, extensive, but falls in a different category. To some extent already in the interwar period, but principally after World War II, development and welfare expenditures by metropolitan governments in the colonies increased.[3] Such policies will not be considered in this paper, which is chiefly concerned with *foreign* assistance, but they did in many cases provide points of departure for the assistance programmes after independence.

Indeed, the concept of "foreign aid to developing nations" had virtually no place in these countries, except as it referred to multilateral aid, until the late 1950's. A systematic inventory of the variety of development and assistance programmes pursued by colonial powers in present and former dependencies was undertaken in response to United Nations and OEEC questionnaires, as the first comprehensive statistics of economic assistance were prepared.[4] The Development Assistance Group, formed in 1960 and in

---

1. John D. Montgomery, *The Politics of Foreign Aid: American Experience in Southeast Asia* (1962), p. 252.
2. *Ibid.*, p. 247.
3. For the U.K., see Overseas Development Institute, *British Aid, 1*, p. 7.
4. A United Nations report on "International economic assistance to underdeveloped countries: statistics of official contributions in 1960" (E/3556) was prepared in response to a resolution by the Economic and Social Council in 1957; the first version of *The Flow of Financial Resources to Countries in Course of Economic Development* covered the years 1956-59 and was published by OECD in 1961.

1961 transformed into the Development Assistance Committee of the OECD, stimulated further attention to economic assistance as a distinct category of operations. In many countries, the first public awareness of the extent and character of such assistance came with the publication of government reports to DAC, which revealed unexpectedly large expenditures of this kind.

When decolonisation is achieved without lacerating rupture, there are numerous forces making for continuity in the economic relationship between the former metropolis and the new countries. Ties of language, culture, and mutual familiarity are of genuine importance. So are the interests of remaining settlers and investors. That these may become sources of serious conflict goes without saying; yet the need for an explicit case for foreign aid is smaller when such continuity exists. The existence and tradition of a colonial service may create a considerable momentum unless diplomatic and economic relationships are severed. Old and established programmes may be spared the opposition reserved for new budgetary appropriations and benefit from the force of tradition. The number of agencies and departments engaged in activities which qualify as "development assistance" tends to be large, and the parliamentary and public debate, therefore, fragmented.

Yet, the relationship between colonial emancipation and foreign aid is not simple. Private and public investment in underdeveloped colonies was concentrated in Asia and North Africa, and investment in Africa south of the Sahara was comparatively modest. In the former regions, independence came earlier and it is notable how little foreign assistance the former metropolitan powers extend there. The reasons vary, but as of now, Indonesia, New Guinea, and the countries in Indo-China receive little or no aid from their mother countries, Morocco and Tunisia only a fraction of their total aid receipts. India and Pakistan do indeed receive British aid in significant amounts, but these too are dwarfed by other aid receipts and on a per capita basis they are trifling compared to British aid in Africa.

It is, in fact, in Africa and specifically in the countries emerging in the second wave of emancipation between 1958 and 1962 that the foreign assistance of European colonial powers is presently concentrated, and this inevitably puts its stamp on the thinking about foreign aid in these countries.

FRANCE

Although none of the components in French assistance have been growing much in recent years, French bilateral assistance remains higher in proportion to her GNP than that of other countries. The total flow of grants, loans, and other expenditures disbursed in 1962 was about 880 million dollars. Of this, about 850 million were directed towards countries in the franc zone, and part of that to the overseas departments and territories still linked to France. These scattered possessions receive almost ten times as much per capita as the beneficiaries of French aid in Africa South of the Sahara, although it amounts to only about 15 per cent of total assistance. If these expenditures are left aside as being in the nature of internal development outlays rather than foreign aid, the picture in 1962 was as indicated on page 28.

The states issuing from Indo-China now receive only token assistance. In Morocco and Tunisia, French financial assistance is limited to a small fraction of that received from other sources (although a large number of

Million Dollars.

	GRANTS	LOANS	CURRENT EXPENDITURES	TOTAL	PER CENT
Algeria	245.9	42.9	82.8	371.6	51
African States (incl. Madagascar)	99.5	24.3	180.0	303.8	42
Morocco and Tunisia	0.2	17.8	24.7	42.7	6
Cambodia, Laos, Viet-Nam	7.9	—	—	7.9	1

French teachers are maintained in those countries). In fact, in the spring of 1964, Tunisian aid was completely suspended in retaliation for the expropriation of French land-holdings. On the other hand, the countries in tropical Africa which attained their independence in the last wave of emancipation have so far remained remarkably close to the metropolis in the aid relationship, sometimes in spite of seriously strained diplomatic relations.[1] It is on these former French possessions in tropical Africa, and on Algeria, that the massive French assistance effort is centered. Outside of this area, French aid is fairly insignificant. In the words of Ambassador Jean Chauvel:

> it is quite clear that, while France makes an enormous effort for some sixty million people, what she devotes to the rest of mankind amounts to very little in comparison.[2]

In such a situation, the motives and reasons for French policy in her own former possessions in Africa are bound to be substantially different from those that might guide her in participation in the assistance of other parts of the underdeveloped world.

THE JEANNENEY REPORT

The so-called Jeanneney Report that appeared in 1963 was nothing less than a major attempt to consider France's present and future policy and co-operation vis-à-vis the underdeveloped world as a whole.[3] French development assistance has so far consisted largely of a variety of activities in formerly dependent territories. Appearing at a time when, in the view of French authorities, the period of "decolonisation" has been completed, the Jeanneney Report may be read as a first inquiry into the question of what post-colonial French foreign aid policy should be.

The report was submitted by a Commission of Inquiry appointed by the government and headed by Professor Jean-Marcel Jeanneney. This procedure, customary in Anglo-Saxon countries and in many parts of Europe, is in itself unusual in France. The Commission was created to advise the Minister in charge of Administration Reform, and part of its mandate was to study the administrative organisation of aid policy. What it recommended on this subject was not included in the published version of the report.

---

1. Guinea may be said to be an exception, but there are signs that even her economic links to France will be resumed.
2. *Jeanneney Report,* II, 43.
3. Ministère d'Etat Chargé de la Réforme Administrative, *La Politique de Coopération avec les Pays en Voie de Développement.* Rapport de la Commission d'Etude instituée par le Décret du 12 mars 1963, remis au Gouvernement le 18 juillet 1963. 2 vols.

The report first of all considered the reasons for a policy of aid or "co-operation" with underdeveloped countries. It firmly rejected the notion that the economic advantages from such a policy would be such as to constitute a valid argument for aid. Among the genuine reasons for a French assistance policy, the first was said to be the simple duty imposed by human solidarity, and the second France's need of "rayonnement" — the diffusion of a civlisation claiming universal validity and the legitime desire of a nation to implant its culture peacefully. More generally, it was also recognised that a policy of co-operation with the new nations might bring certain diplomatic and other advantages, however diffuse and uncertain. The French interest in friendly relations with underdeveloped countries in general merged with a shared Western interest in averting the formation of a world-wide bloc of hostile nations. But aid must not become an instrument of the cold war; it must aim at strengthening the developing nations; it must recognise their freedom to find their own political personality and to preserve their political independence (I, 47).

France was also regarded as in some respects particularly well equipped to pursue a policy of co-operation with the new nations. Her revolutionary tradition would find wider appeal with the end of her colonial involvements, and the very smallness of France in a world of giant powers would reassure both receiving countries and other donors. A French presence in the underdeveloped world might thus serve to enhance stability.

So far, however, French aid policy has been overwhelmingly concentrated on the French-speaking states in Africa, and the central question in the report might well be said to be the relation between this kind of assistance to countries where French aid was expected to continue to play a preponderant part, and French assistance in countries where France would not be the dominant donor.

The Commission concluded that French aid to Africa should enjoy continued priority although an increasing share of French foreign aid should be distributed to other parts of the world. Behind this conclusion was the view that the objectives of French aid were necessarily different in Africa and elsewhere. In the African economies where French assistance fundamentally affects the course of economic development, the objective should be to strengthen the economic independence of the new nations, and the assistance programme should be substantial enough to meet vital needs when they will not be covered by multilateral aid, other donors, or self-help. The Commission was dissatisfied with the large role of budgetary and administrative support in the former dependencies. In the new states in Indochina, and in Morocco and Tunisia, French aid is now virtually limited to the educational field, but in Africa south of the Sahara. French administrators continue to play an important and, in the view of the Jeanneney Report, an excessive role, and much of the French aid has been allocated to the support of administrative and governmental expenses which began to exceed public revenues already before independence as the result of development projects involving large recurrent costs.

Although the total capital requirements in the African states are expected to be very high in the coming decade, it was hoped that a growing share would be supplied through the Development Fund of the European Economic Community, and French aid to Africa was therefore not expected to grow rapidly. If continued economic growth in France makes greater resources available for foreign assistance, they should rather be channelled into other parts of the world of greater political urgency and into areas offering more rapidly expanding markets to French industry than impoverished Africa.

The report envisaged a gradual "rapprochement" of the type of aid extented inside and outside the franc zone, with a shift away from budgetary assistance and grants towards lending and credit guarantees inside the zone. Outside the zone, it expected a softening of terms of lending, necessitated in part by the problem of indebtedness :

> If the aid which over the years has been given to developing countries in the form of grants had been furnished in the form of ordinary loans, the contributions they receive today would hardly suffice to meet the burden of interest and amortisation payments. (I, 92)

The report stressed the difficulties of evolving a coherent policy vis-à-vis the underdeveloped countries at large without a consolidation of the administration of foreign aid. Although its proposals in this respect were not published, they have been summarised by the Prime Minister and amounted to putting all foreign aid operations under the Ministry of Foreign Affairs, assisted by a number of Secretariats.

The smallness of the French contributions outside the franc zone seemed to dictate a measure of co-operation with other donors. Insofar as such co-operation would take the form of multilateral action, the Jeanneney Report emphasised that France should secure an influence in the respective organisations consonant with her contribution. It expressed a preference for small multilateral groups on account of their greater flexibility, and suggested that the operations of the EEC Development Fund might be extended to all developing countries. It would combine the efficiency of bilateral aid with the greater resources of joint action and make Europe a powerful factor in foreign aid and "might contribute to offset the preponderance which the United States gains from her heavy participation in the World Bank and her direct aid to the *tiers monde*". (I, 93)

The possibilities of a bilateral aid strategy in the world outside of the African states to which it is now concentrated were exhaustively discussed by Ambassador Jean Chauvel, one of the members of the Commission, in a memorandum included in the separate volume of studies and reports on special aspects of foreign aid. Here French aid was viewed as a diplomatic instrument for influence which should not, however, be scattered too thinly. Where it could neither make a significant contribution, nor play a diplomatic role, it should not be attempted. Thus, a French effort in India and Pakistan seemed to be of low priority, while the possibilities of significant results were greater in the Middle East, especially where the French language retains a hold, and in South America. A French aid offensive in Latin America would offer a way of improving the political conditions for the success of the American aid effort by reducing the exclusive dependence on the United States of Latin American recipients. (II, 41) The foreign aid policies of other countries were briefly contrasted with those of France : United States aid was described as in its origins humanitarian but politically oriented as the result of the Soviet response. British aid was partly genuine co-operation, partly a tool of prudent national expansion. German, Italian and Japanese assistance policies largely served purposes of economic expansion. It was recognised that in her aid policy vis-à-vis the underdeveloped world at large where she is not responding to the special circumstances that prevail in the French speaking African states, France too will orient her bilateral assistance partly by commercial criteria. (II, 44)

The report touched upon some of the questions of commercial policy vis-à-vis the underdeveloped countries and recommended that France should propose and support policies of commodity price stabilisation, as such policies spare the political sensibilities of recipients and escape the suspicions and frictions to which closer involvement in their economies give rise. The report favoured a system of tariff preferences for manufactures exported by developing countries, and it stressed the necessity of providing reasonable security for foreign private investors in developing countries.

In the relatively lively debate of French aid policy following the publication of the Jeanneney Report, French aid to Africa has rarely been questioned in principle.

The case for it is couched in terms of the historical and moral responsibility specific to France in these countries, when it is not, as in the government's report on the first five years of the policy of "co-operation", simply taken for granted. The policy of co-operation is there presented simply as the continuation of colonial efforts to promote economic development. Although co-operation is said to have replaced the idea of assimilation and economic complementary, the Ministry of Co-operation claims also to defend French national interests and secure "tangible counterparts" while serving the cause of the aided countries.[1]

Public criticism of the French assistance programme focuses on its volume, forms, techniques, administration, and occasionally on the excessive concentration on Africa, but rarely on the principle that the French speaking states in Africa should be helped. The position that comes closest to rejecting this principle is the much publicised one of M. Raymond Cartier, who opened his campaign against the French colonial system in 1956 on the grounds that it was an excessive drain on French ressources and impeded French modernisation, and now directs his fire against foreign assistance to the old possessions which is turning out to be even more costly.[2] The *cartierist* attack describes the aid as largely wasted and as serving to maintain dubious but profligate governments rather than to promote economic development. On the other hand, it underscores the urgent needs for development and modernisation in France herself: the need for teachers and schools, hospitals, housing, and accelerated industrial investment.

Similar arguments have been forcefully presented by Senator Bonnefous in an extensive criticism of the wastefulness of the aid programme presently pursued, and in the debate following the publication of the Jeanneney report. Insofar as they merely focus on alleged instances of evident maladministration, these criticisms cannot be said to add up to a distinct aid doctrine. Any publicly financed programme stands under the sinister suspicion of being wasteful. As in all other aid-giving countries, reports of sumptuous extravagance and corruption in receiving countries are cited in criticism of the French aid programme, often coupled with the complaint that the aid is not only economically but also politically waisted. Surveys of French public attitudes to the foreign aid programme undertaken in 1962 and 1964 showed

---

1. Ministère de la Coopération, *1959-1964 — Cinq ans de Fonds d'Aide et de Coopération*, p. 15.
2. M. Cartier is the publisher of *Paris Match*; his recent articles on French foreign aid appeared on February 29, March 3, and March 14, 1964.

that *cartierist* propositions are the most widely held *negative* views of such aid — but also that such views are usually associated with the position that aid is excessive rather than that it should be abandoned.[1]

The criticism on this point is confined to financial assistance. As seems to be the case in most countries, technical assistance has greater public appeal in France, and this is particularly true of that part of this effort that consists in promotion of the French language and French culture generally. On the desirability of such work, there seems to be no disagreement at all, if allowance is made for the occasional doubt whether the French school system can spare the 30,000 teachers maintained overseas.

The desire to strengthen the position of the French language in the world is sometimes presented as more than a reason to give educational and technical assistance. It is thus used as an argument for an emphasis on bilateral assistance in general. This point was bluntly made by Prime Minister Pompidou in one of the rare parliamentary debates about the foreign aid problem as a whole. Recognising that especially UNESCO used numerous French-speaking experts, he continued :

> It nevertheless remains tone that multilateral aid, as it is handled by the large international organisations, leads to a strengthening of the position of the English language. But, I repeat, for us Frenchmen it is somehow a need to defend the French tongue. This is a fundamental reason to maintain bilateral aid[2].

However, the Prime Minister also criticised multilateral aid as "necessarily more rigid, more abstract, more technocratic and more ambitious than the bilateral form". In this he expressed a position more sharply articulated in France than elsewhere, notably by the Ministry of Co-operation in its championing of the bilateral relationship. In its 1964 report, it suggested that attempts at co-ordination of French aid with other assistance efforts encountered serious obstacles :

> They meet with a resistance originating either in the narrowly nationalist views of certain states or in the opposition of certain specialised international organisations. The former see in the assistance to the *tiers-monde* merely an opportunity to promote their trade and secure market outlets. The latter uphold, sometimes against all evidence, principles of action which could only lead the underdeveloped countries to stagnation o rchronic deficits.[3]

Multilateral aid was termed a flight from responsibility, in danger of turning into sterile and "babelisé" technocracy committed to erroneous doctrines :

> Multilateral aid can and should develop... if those who are charged with its management do not make themselves the spokesmen for obsolescent orthodoxy or the unavowed representatives of a group of nations.[4]

Effective assistance policy, it was suggested, requires a more intimate relationship of "cooperation", dialogue, and sharing of responsibility between aiding and aided.

---

1. See Ch. III.
2. Assemblée Nationale, 10 June, 1964. *Journal Officiel*, p. 1785.
3. Ministère de la Coopération, *Cinq ans de Fonds d'Aide et de Coopération*, p. 57.
4. *Ibid.*, p. 60.

An aid philosophy of this kind is understandable in the special relationship between France and the African states which is the responsibility of the Ministry of Co-operation. But one of the major questions posed for French assistance policy is whether it should in the future be redirected towards other parts of the world in which France has no such special position.

Such a redirection was recommended in the Jeanneney report and the French government has declared its intention to reduce progressively its aid to its traditional recipients and increase its assistance to other countries. It has also declared that its policy will be to keep the total volume of aid at its present absolute level, so that the burden relative to GNP will decline somewhat.[1],

But a policy of aid to the *tiers monde* at large, which in the internationalist conception of assistance policy may be described as a mere step towards a more equitable distribution of French aid, poses a host of essentially new problems. The motives for a bilateral aid of this sort, the criteria for its allocation, the forms in which it should be given, and the ways in which it should be administered, will all appear radically different. A new philosophy of aid will be required, based on a view of the international scene at large and France's place in it.

Senator Bonnefous finds it desirable that bilateral aid should gradually disappear, except in the realm of technical and cultural assistance, and sees the problem of aid to the *tiers monde* at large as an international rather than a French problem, and, therefore, one suited for multilateral organisation[2]. It is, however, clear that the French government regards foreign assistance as an instrument of foreign policy which is to be used to fortify the political and economic ties between France and other countries. But such assistance — as the credits already granted to Greece, Turkey, and Spain, and in Latin-America show — will be of a new character, and it is safe to say that many of the features that have come to be thought of as typical of French assistance will not be present. Grants and general programme aid are not likely to be given to countries without a special relationship with France, and assistance is more likely to be linked to specific French export expansion, and to diplomatic objectives.

Sor far, the problems of an aid policy towards the *tiers monde* at large rather than former dependencies have not become the subject of much debate in France. They have been overshadowed by the preoccupation aroused by the fact that France's aid expenditures have seemed such a heavy burden in comparison with other countries. However, if present trends continue, the volume of French assistance may soon be more comparable to others, and France will also find herself faced with problems of aid policy far more similar to those that other countries have confronted.

THE UNITED KINGDOM

In Britain, as in France, aid to poor regions has its roots in colonial policy, and the evolution of British aid may actually be described as a continuous widening of the sphere within which assistance has been thought a legitimate policy.

---

1. M. Pompidou in the Assembly on June 10, 1964. *Journal Officiel*, p. 1785.
2. *Les Milliards qui s'envolent* (Paris, 1963), p. 244.

Traditional doctrine expected colonial government to be self-supporting and meet the costs of government as well as development out of local revenue. If a dependency went into the red, grants-in-aid were given and the Treasury in London assumed control of its finances. The gradual recognition of the need for outside help to develop the colonial territories in the mutual interest of Britain and the subject populations is often traced back to Joseph Chamberlain, but the Colonial Development Act of 1929 was the first to provide regular funds specifically for the development of the colonies. Such direct assistance, however, was until 1950 reserved for dependent territories "lacking responsible government". India, Burma, and Southern Rhodesia were thus not eligible for assistance under this Act, nor under the subsequent Colonial Development and Welfare Act of 1940[1].

The underlying view was that Exchequer funds should be spent only where the United Kingdom was responsible and the Treasury thus accountable for their uses, and that it did not, in the words of Mr. Oliver Stanley, "foster a feeling of self-reliance... that it should be possible for a responsible self-governing colony to draw upon funds of this nature"[2].

Although in 1950 it was recognised that it might be undesirable to reward progress towards responsible government by exclusion from development assistance, it remained accepted doctrine that independent members of the Commonwealth could not be financially aided. Although development assistance grew rapidly in the postwar years, until 1957 virtually none of it was given to such independent countries.

In the late 1950's, the emancipation of many of the African colonies and the sudden awareness of the need for external assistance to India made for a change in this respect, and in 1958 it was announced at the Commonwealth Trade and Economic Conference at Montreal that development aid would be extended to independent members of the Commonwealth. Since then, an increasing share of British bilateral aid — now about one-half — has gone to such countries. At the same time, Britain does not provide more than one-third of the aid to Commonwealth countries. The British aid system has become more aligned with others and increasingly a part of the international assistance effort. In the 1960's even a number of non-Commonwealth countries without special historical links with Britain have come to receive financial assistance.

The transition from colonial assistance to a new conception of aid policy is thus of very recent date. This is reflected in the three White Papers in which, since 1957, the government has presented the official view of the objectives of British aid policy. The 1957 paper on *The United Kingdom's Role in Commonwealth Development* still rejected the use of public funds to assist independent countries, except in "very special circumstances"[3]. The special responsibility recognised towards colonies

> ceases when they achieve independence. The Government, therefore, does not envisage government to government loans as a normal means of assisting such countries. Their interests can better be served if they build up their own credit.

---

1. Malta was excluded until the suspension of parliamentary government in 1933 made her eligible. Cf. ODI, *British Aid*, 5, p. 8.
2. House of Commons, 24th January, 1946, Vol. 432, Col. 532 ; cited in ODI, *British Aid* 5, p. 8.
3. Cmnd. 237.

The greatest emphasis was laid on the role of private capital:

It is through the investment of privately owned funds that the United Kingdom has made its most valuable contribution to development in other Commonwealth countries, and Her Majesty's Government considers that this should continue.

Written between two serious balance of payments crises, the White Paper of 1957 also stressed the limited margin for capital exports and the importance of the "strength of sterling".

It was a year later that the United Kingdom, at the Montreal Conference, announced its new policy of extending certain development loans to independent members of the Commonwealth, and by 1960 British aid policy had changed even further. The White Paper of 1960 was submitted by the Chancellor of the Exchequer rather than, as in 1957, by the Secretary of State for Commonwealth Relations, and dealt with *Assistance from the United Kingdom for Overseas Development*[1]. The title reflects its broader concern with less developed countries at large, and the paper was largely devoted to government aid since "many of the poorer countries cannot under present conditions attract all the private capital they need". Here for the first time the responsibility of the advanced countries to aid the less developed countries was declared to be a basis of UK policy, and in its comprehensive view of such assistance the paper expressed the new conception of development assistance which also was to mark the 1963 paper on *Aid to Developing Countries*.

THE BRITISH WHITE PAPER

This White Paper[2] was presented to Parliament in September, 1963, by the Chief Secretary of the Treasury, in order to outline the changes in economic aid policy over the previous three years and to describe Britain's aid effort.

It recalled the increasing gap between the standards of living in industrialised and developing nations and the responsibility to help the developing countries. The purpose of promoting development by means of aid was said to be "to help to buttress stability in the developing countries", and economic progress in developing countries should also "eventually be to the benefit of the donor countries as well" (p. 5).

It placed foreign aid in a long perspective and suggested that although it "is likely to be no more than a passing phase in the history of the world", the aid era was not, therefore, likely to be short, indeed its end is not in sight.

The total British aid programme had doubled between 1957/8 and 1961/2, as disbursements on grants and loans rose from 81 million pounds to 160 million. That the increase was not uniform is seen from the distribution in these two years (p. 15):

Although the number of colonies was considerably smaller in the latter period, more than half the increase actually fell in this category. As the White Paper commented:

---

1. Cmnd., 947.
2. Cmnd. 2147.

	1957/58	1961/62
		£ Million.
Bilateral aid:		
Colonial territories	47.3	95.5
Independent Commonwealth	4.7	44.5
Other countries	10.3	13.8
Multilateral aid	18.8	6.3
Total aid	81.1	160.1

The geographical distribution of our aid expenditure is influenced by our history. Our aid programme can be said to have started as part of the discharge of our responsibilities to the dependent territories, and although many of these territories are now independent, nearly half of our expenditure (in 1962/63) is devoted to the diminishing number for which we still have direct responsibility (p. 16).

A very large increase was also recorded for independent Commonwealth countries :

> Having helped these countries to political independence, it is a natural and fitting continuation of the earlier relationship that we should now assist them in their efforts to achieve balanced and self-sustaining economies (p. 16).

The two remaining categories fared worse, but the fall in the multilateral contribution largely reflects the end of drawings by the IBRD. Although, in the words of the white paper, "there are a number of foreign (non-Commonwealth) countries whose special relationship with us we have recognised by helping their economic development", the bilateral aid to such countries increased only modestly and fell in relative importance. Of these countries, many had close historical links with Britain without being members of the Commonwealth, e.g. Jordan, Libya, Sudan, and Nepal.

The amounts that Britain could spend on aid to developing countries was said to depend "primarily on the state of our balance of payments, because of the substantial charge that overseas expenditure imposes on this balance", but also on the trend in public expenditure as a whole, and on whether aid was tied or untied and on the terms on which it was given (p. 12).

As in France, UK assistance is given in a great variety of ways, many of which are specifically destined for colonies and former dependencies. They include :

i) Budgetary grants and technical assistance grants (on "departmental votes") ;
ii) Colonial Development and Welfare Act loans and grants ;
iii) Exchequer loans to colonial governments, approved in 1959 as funds available in the London market for colonial issues were inadequate ;
iv) Loans under the Export Guarantees Act.

The White Paper was essentially an account of these varied operations that make up the British "aid effort". It contained no recommendations or criticisms, but on certain points it expressed the position of the British Government. On the subject of tied aid, the United Kingdom would be ready to take part in an international move towards untying of aid :

Provided that British industry remained competitive, and that we were contributing no more than our due share of aid, we would benefit if all aid were untied, and the developing nations would also benefit, by being able to place their contracts in the most economic source of supply (p. 13).

The British Government had also decided on a number of steps to make aid available on easier terms when the situation of the recipient made this desirable. In the past, the general principle was to reserve grants for colonial territories and to give other aid in the form of loans, but now grants are occasionally made to newly independent countries as well. British long-term loans had previously been given for a maximum of 25 years, with a grace period of seven years for repayment of principal, and at interest rates equal to those at which the government borrows in the domestic market plus a service charge. In the White Paper, it announced its readiness to extend loans for up to 30 years, with grace periods of up to ten years. Instead of a direct reduction of the interest rate it proposed, "where the economic circumstances of the recipient country make it necessary", to waive interest as well as repayment during a grace period of seven years, which would bring down the effective rate of interest significantly.

As in France, parliamentary discussion of aid remained fragmented by the lingering division of responsibility among many government departments and there was relatively little public debate of the implications of the new look for aid policy. Government documentation was also sparse, although the non-governmental Overseas Development Institute, set up in 1960, has contributed significantly to the knowledge of the British aid programme and posed vital issues[1].

However, in October, 1964, a Ministry for Overseas Development was created by the new government, under a Cabinet Minister, and charged with more extensive responsibilities in the aid field than most comparable agencies. The Ministry assumed functions previously discharged by the Overseas Department, by the Department of Technical Co-operation and by the Treasury, and one of its first tasks was precisely to review the aid programme in the light of the specific exigencies of development assistance. Emerging in the midst of yet another balance of payments crisis, the new Ministry must face these issues in unfavourable circumstances, but the unanimously favourable reception of this reorganisation suggests that British aid is entering a phase of constructive consolidation.

GERMANY

Without any relevant background in colonial development efforts, German development assistance belongs almost entirely to the recent years in which the "modern conception of aid to developing nations has been adopted. Appropriations for technical assistance were made in 1956, and increasing amounts of financial assistance to underdeveloped countries were granted in the late 1950's. Already from the start it grew very rapidly, and it is quite evenly distributed.[2]

---

1. Overseas Development Institute, *British Aid — A Factual Survey,* 5 pamphlets (London, 1963-64).
2. See Chapter IV.

By and large, the motives for German aid have not been questioned and restated so much as the forms. No strategic or security considerations are given much weight, and no historic ties of any importance have guided the direction of aid. The poverty of the underdeveloped world and the social and political instability assumed to be related to this poverty tend to be evoked by government spokesmen, with stress on the moral obligation to help and occasional reference to the prudent self-interest of doing so. Repeatedly, the present Minister for Economic Co-operation, Herr Scheel, has described it as "welfare policy on an international scale".[1] No attempt is usually made to show development assistance to be positively in the German national interest, although it has been suggested by a German business organisation that one should not "shrink away from mentioning the interests of industrial and capital exporting countries by their name, e.g. the need to secure market outlets and to locate labour intensive production in the developing countries".[2] On the other hand, the government has frequently been attacked for pursuing a policy of export promotion in the guise of development assistance. This it has consistently denied, stressing in earlier years its adherence to the principle of united aid[3]. It has, on occasion, made reference to the common responsibility of the industrial countries vis-à-vis the developing ones and to the co-operation in DAG and DAC[4].

In the parliamentary debates about the assistance policy, the opposition has not questioned the basic assumptions as, in the words of a Socialist deputy in 1962:

In this house, we have no further need to talk about the need and motives for German development assistance and German aid policy[5].

That foreign aid is not however, an ordinary political issue is well illustrated by the unusual measure of agreement that, if public opinion is unfavourable to the aid programme, it needs to be better informed and funds must be appropriated to enlighten it[6].

German aid doctrine has from the outset been more specific on the subject of the forms of aid, and it differs most prominently from those of other countries in its approach to private investment. In other donor countries, the assumption has increasingly come to be that foreign aid is necessary because private capital movements do not in to-day's situation suffice to meet the need for development finance. The role of private investment is not ignored, but the difference between investments arising, as it were, from normal trade, and genuine aid measures is recognised as fundamental. In German aid philosophy, on the other hand, private investment is frequently described as the most desirable type of "aid", and the promotion of private investment is given high priority. It is surely a misnomer, however, to refer to private investment as "private assistance"; to the extent that it is induced

---

1. E.g. In his lecture at the Deutscher Überseetag, Hamburg, May 7, 1962.
2. DIHT, *Tätigkeitsbericht* für 1963.
3. E.g. Dr. Erhard, then Minister of Economics, in a broadcast in May, 1961. *Handbuch der Entwicklungshilfe,* II A 30, p. 52.
4. Dr. Erhard in the Bundestag, May 5, 1961.
5. Herr Wichnewski (SPD), 49. Sitzung des Deutschen Bundestages am 16 November, 1962.
6. Cf. e.g., Foreign Minister von Brentano in the Bundestag, May 5, 1961; all speakers in the Bundestag November 16, 1962; Herr Scheel at the Berlin meeting of the International Public Relations Association, May 30, 1963.

by tax privileges and government guarantees of export credits and investments, there is an element of official assistance involved, but even then it cannot be assumed that this will benefit the borrower or capital importer rather than the investor.

In any case, German aid policy has in doctrine — though less in actual fact — centered on private investment. The extensive report submitted by the Council of Economic Advisors to the Ministry of Economics in 1960 about "rational economic assistance" stressed in the first place the urgency of checking the capital flight from many underdeveloped countries, secondly the importance of promoting private investment[1]. Indeed, it followed that the entire German balance-of-payments surplus might be regarded as so much aid, at least insofar as it consisted of capital exports to the less developed countries.

The advisors recognised that the need for financing of infrastructure projects called for government lending or grants. They expressed a preference for loans, as these impose financial discipline on the borrower, do not violate his national pride, and involve a smaller sacrifice. They thought, however, that in principle government loans and grants should be administered multilaterally. In this respect, the official position has come to be another — in the words of Herr Scheel, "multilateral as much as necessary, bilateral as much as possible[2]" — but otherwise the principles laid down by the advisory council constituted a basis for an aid programme. To this was later added a sharp preference for project aid. Programme assistance was in principle to be extended only in cases of internationally co-ordinated actions and where careful controls were possible. Budgetary assistance was strictly excluded[3]. Credits were to be preferred over grants because they made for a better aid relationship, for "partnership" rather than almstaking. Credit, moreover, should so far as possible be on commercial terms; apprehension about the excessive indebtedness of many underdeveloped countries has led to a modification but not the abandonment of this principle[4]. Grants are to be used only for technical assistance.

In 1961, the Foreign Minister declared that German public aid was to be given only in response to requests, without any political conditions, and with respect for the political independence of the recipient. But he added:

> It must be said clearly that decisions about the type, extent, and direction of our development aid very largely must be determined by political considerations[5].

The fact that it was given without political strings "does not, of course, mean that we pay no attention to the political attitude... of the countries that request assistance".

In the government message to the Bundestag in November, 1961, the section on development assistance was, in fact, preceded by an expression of

---

1. Gutachten des wissenschaftlichen Beirates beim Bundeswirtschaftsministerium über eine rationelle Wirtschaftshilfe an die Entwicklungsländer. In *Handbuch der Entwicklungshilfe,* II A 30.
2. In his speech on May 7, 1962, at Hamburg.
3. Declaration by Dr. Erhard, read by Dr. Westrick in the Bundestag, May 5, 1961.
4. See, e.g., the lecture by Staatssekretär Dr. Westrick in Essen, October 19, 1961; *Handbuch der Entwicklungshilfe,* II A 30, p. 71.
5. Herr von Brentano in the Bundestag, May 5, 1961.

gratitude to the number of Asian, Latin American and African states which in the United Nations and elsewhere had favoured the reunification of Germany[1]. The principle of "friends first", i.e. the application of the Hallstein doctrine to the field of foreign aid, was frequently re-stated in subsequent years, but it was not until 1964 and 1965 that it was put to the test, particularly as the result of development in Tanzania and Egypt, which served as a sharp reminder that foreign aid is not an effective instrument for short-term diplomacy.

These developments coincide with the onset of a mood of doubt and questioning, and with rising criticism and disenchantment in certain quarters and although the flow of German public assistance has continued to rise, there has been attrition in the commitments and the budgetary appropriations in the last years. At the same time, however, German aid practice has undisputably evolved to greater maturity.

When the Ministry for Economic Co-operation was established in 1961, this was a token of the will to replace ad hoc measures by a more systematic policy, and the responsibilities of this Ministry have been enlarged in later years, although the Ministry of Economics retains charge of capital aid. The principles laid down by the new Ministry were understandably for the most part not novel, but it is no exaggeration to say that gradually a doctrine with a new slant has emerged.

The distribution of aid received more attention. At first, the lack of historical ties had been conceived as a freedom to pursue a pragmatic policy, but a general dispersion of aid was found unsuitable, and in 1962 Herr Scheel announced a policy of "moving foci of concentration" (*wandernde Schwerpunkte*), "roughly along the lines: yesterday the Middle East, today Africa, today and tomorrow Latin America[2]". Although technical assistance is widely dispersed, financial assistance is concentrated as far as possible.

That the efforts and achievements of developing countries themselves are more important than any measure of foreign aid is stressed in all assistance programmes, but in the 1962 reappraisal of German policy it was felt that self-help should be made into a decision criteria for the extension of development assistance. In the past, the requirements of self-help had provided the rationale for such practices as supplying only foreign exchange requirements of a project and leaving local cost to be covered by the host country[3].

New and greater emphasis was put on human development, on technical assistance, education and training, on welfare measures (*Sozialhilfe*)[4], and also on the need to promote entrepreneurship and small business in developing countries.

Moreover, the insistence on tying aid to specific projects has been modified by the recognition of the need for "maintenance support" to finance a broader range of imports, and attention to comprehensive pro-

---

1. Read by Dr. Erhard on behalf of Dr. Adenauer in the Bundestag, November 29, 1961.
2. Speech in Hamburg, May 7, 1962. The objections to the *Giesskannenschema*, like the French dissatisfaction with *saupoudrage*, seemed to be the suspicion that no lasting effects could be reached on a small scale.
3. Staatssekretär Vialon, speech in Stuttgart, June 29, 1962. *Handbuch der Entwicklungshilfe*, II A 30, p. 114.
4. "With its objective to reduce social tensions in the developing countries, German development assistance has undoubtedly for some time now found a decisively new orientation." Staatssekretär Vialon, 29 June, 1962.

grammes of development planning, rather than isolated projects, is given increasing stress.

To summarise: in German aid policy, the considerations of security and long-term diplomatic strategy, which have been prominent in the U.S. discussion, have been of little effective significance, although foreign aid is recognised as being ineluctably an instrument in German foreign policy. Nor is German aid dictated by lingering responsibilities of interests in dependent territories. Instead, German aid philosophy, as expounded in justification of the assistance policy, is dominated by two strands of thought: the plight of the underdeveloped countries calls for a German sacrifice in the interest of "international welfare policy", but simultaneously it is repeatedly asserted that strictly commercial relations, and especially private investment, constitute a superior mode of assistance. In actual fact, German private investment in less developed countries has, in spite of many measures of encouragement, remained stagnant in recent years, while there has been a great surge in official assistance, mostly in the form of lending. As elsewhere, the term "aid" is frequently eschewed in favour of "co-operation" or "partnership", but inevitably tension persists between the conception of assistance as involving a measure of sacrifice, and a partnership based essentially on commercial terms and mutual advantage[1].

BELGIUM

The smaller colonial powers of Europe seem in different ways to be confronting problems similar to those of France and Britain in their search for an aid philosophy. The Belgian assistance effort is concentrated on Congo (Leopoldville), and to a lesser extent on Rwanda and Burundi, and it is anticipated that future aid will continue to be directed mostly to these countries. Yet, the issue of a more general assistance policy has been raised and continues to be under consideration. A general survey was published already in 1959 by a study group appointed by the Belgian Royal Institute of International Affairs[2].

In the essay addressing itself to the specific role of Belgium in the *tiers monde,* it was argued that, as Belgium had neither the means nor the aims of the great powers and could not undertake massive direct assistance, it should "conduct bilateral relations as economic and social co-operation but reserve for international organisation whatever might have the character of a free gift[3]. Co-operation should be founded on joint interests, essentially commercial, and the choice of partners should be guided by this need: "We must choose those whose economy, when developed through joint efforts, will give rise to the most profitable flows of trade for the Belgian economy[4]."

So far, however, the transition from the colonial system dominates the composition of Belgian aid, in which by far the largest item is the charge on the old Congolese external debt guaranteed by Belgium. The rest consists

---

1. See, e.g., Samuel Karres, "Partnerschaft oder Geschäft mit den Entwicklungsländern ?", in *Probleme der Entwicklungshilfe,* Schriftenreihe der Friedrich-Ebert-Stiftung (1963), p. 38.
2. *La Belgique et l'aide économique aux pays sous-développés* (Brussels, 1959).
3. Jean-Louis Servais, "Le rôle de la Belgique dans le monde sous-développé de l'avenir", in *La Belgique et l'aide...,* p. 435.
4. *Loc. cit.*

largely of technical assistance in the form of the maintenance of over 2,000 experts in the Congo and in Rwanda and Burundi, roughly half of whom were teachers. In 1963, the structure of Belgian bilateral assistance was:

Million Dollars.

	GRANTS	LOANS
Development projects and balance of payments support in Congo, Rwanda and Burundi	2.3	1.8
Technical Co-operation	23.6	
Consortia loans to Turkey, Yugoslavia and Greece		7.0
Miscellaneous (mainly the charge on the Congo external public debt)	48.9	
	75.8	8.8

The servicing of the old Congolese debt certainly relieves the new state of a burden from the past, which would be very heavy if the debt were to be honoured by the Congo itself. M. Brasseur, the Belgian Minister of Commerce, has described it as

indispensable for the maintenance of the international creditworthiness of the Congo and thus for her possibilities of future development[1].

However this arrangement is regarded, it is clear that only a fraction of Belgian bilateral assistance results in direct involvement in development efforts even in the former colonies. The intention of broadening the Belgian assistance effort and "to open new vistas for Belgian influence (*rayonnement*) in the world[2]" has been voiced repeatedly in the course of the last few years, and machinery for the formulation and implementation of such a policy was created in 1962 in the form of a Ministerial Committee, a consultative council and an *Office de la coopération au développement*. Modest programmes of Belgian technical assistance have already been initiated in a number of countries, but, as indicated by M. Brasseur at the time of the establishment of the new institutions, the search for a general assistance policy vis-a-vis the *tiers monde* raises the question of what kinds of bilateral financial assistance, if any, would be appropriate besides Belgium's multilateral contributions.

THE NETHERLANDS

The same question has arisen in the Netherlands, whose direct development expenditure was until recently largely a matter of colonial spending. The severing of the links with the principal colonies led to the suspension of such expenditure. Thus, in 1963, the change in status of Western New Guinea reduced Dutch bilateral disbursements by almost two-thirds below 1962. In August, 1964, it was announced that sizeable export credits (up to 100 million florins) would be made available to Indonesia in the coming year. This marked the resumption of regular economic relations with that country, but not an intention to supply genuine bilateral development assistance.

---

1. "La politique belge de coopération avec les pays en développement", d'après un discours prononcé par Maurice Brasseur, Ministre du Commerce Extérieur et de l'Assistance Technique, *Textes et Documents,* No. 161, février 1963, Services de l'Information du Ministère des Affaires Etrangères et du Commerce Extérieur, Bruxelles, page 5.
2. *Ibid.,* p. 7.

On the level of principle, the Dutch government has consistently expressed its preference for multilateral rather than bilateral assistance to areas outside the Kingdom ever since, in April, 1956, it first expressed its motives for engaging in an assistance policy. It then took the view that only large countries were capable of genuine financial assistance, but considered the Netherlands in a position to make valuable contributions to the transfer of knowledge, especially in the framework of multilateral technical assistance. In August, 1962, Foreign Minister Luns presented a memorandum on aid to less developed countries to the Dutch Parliament, in which this position was reasserted and elaborated. Three reasons were given for the priority accorded unilateral assistance:

i) Multilateral aid is given in an international framework in which donors and participants alike participate.

ii) The Netherlands is too small to give bilateral aid on a large scale. Only a very limited number of countries could receive such aid, which might influence our relations with other countries unfavourably, as we do not have such areas of interest as England in the Commonwealth, or France in the Community. There is also the danger that we would come under political and economic pressure to give more aid than our capacity allows.

iii) As a small country, we do not possess the political weight and the administrative machinery that would enable us to supervise effectively the rational and economic use of our aid in the receiving countries[1].

The 1962 memorandum did suggest that, in consortia and co-ordinating groups, bilateral contributions take on multilateral aspects and, since 1962, the Dutch assistance programme has, in fact, turned to such solutions. The Dutch government has joined eight international consortia and consultative groups and its bilateral assistance (outside of Surinam and the Netherlands Antilles) consists almost entirely of contributions made in these contexts. These were in the form of loans from the Herstelbank, which raised its funds in the private capital market and the terms were not especially soft, interest rates being $5 - 5\frac{1}{2}$ per cent and maturities generally 25 years. On this point, the 1962 memorandum stated:

> The government is of the opinion that bilateral financial assistance to areas outside the Kingdom on exceptionally favourable terms for the debtor country cannot be considered for the Netherlands. It holds the view that, in principal, the multilateral method only is acceptable for this form of assistance.

The Dutch government seems to have been unreceptive to the suggestion that bilateral assistance should be used to support Dutch exports and, on this score, it has attracted criticism from admirers of, for instance, the German aid system. In the words of Professor Hanrath: "If we are to give away money, then let us do it as much as possible in our own interest[2]." Criticism is also directed against the Dutch contribution to the Development Fund of

---

1. "Memorandum on Aid to Less Developed Countries", presented by Foreign Minister J. Luns to the Second Chamber of the Estates General, 18th August, 1962.
2. Paper prepared for the Annual Meeting of the Dutch Society for Industry and Trade, Haarlem, 13th June, 1962.

the EEC as being merely support of former French colonies; the Government itself in the memorandum of 1962 called this undesirable.

Italy

The flow of Italian public funds to less developed countries contains grants which have stayed around a level of 25-30 million dollars for over a decade, and hard-term loans, which have increased rapidly in the late 1950's and early 1960's.

The bulk of the grants have gone to Somalia as budgetary support, technical assistance, etc. Reparations to Yugoslavia and Ethiopia have until now accounted for a considerable part of the rest. The training of foreign students from less developed countries and technical assistance programmes in North African and Near Eastern countries have played a marginal role in the aid programme, quantitatively speaking.

Loans have been financed through the capital market and terms have been stiff, although a budgetary appropriation now enables the Government to make loans on concessionary terms. The average rate of interest in recent years has been 6-7 per cent, the maturity 6-8 years. Over one-third of recent loan commitments have, in fact, concerned the refinancing of old debts. The remainder consists partly of export credits, partly of contributions to the OECD consortia for Turkey and Greece and untied loans to Tunisia, Egypt and Ethiopia.

The Italian aid programme is not the subject of lively debate in Italy, but it is clear that both long and short run economic considerations reduce the eagerness to engage large resources in it. In view of the development problems faced in the south of the country, Italy is not regarded as a natural exporter of capital, and the serious balance of payments disequilibrium has led to a scaling down of commitments. The programme is concentrated in the Mediterranean and to countries which have an immediate interest to Italy. In Somalia, the Italian involvement is still very great, and there the participation in the development effort is extensive; elsewhere Italian foreign aid strikes a balance between the desire to further political and commercial ties and that of avoiding undue dispersion. To the extent that it takes the form of hard loans, the latter part of the programme involves no serious long-term sacrifice of real resources. Although development assistance is an accepted element of Italian foreign policy, there seems to have been no inquiry into the principles which should guide it until an internal working group was appointed in 1964 to study the problem.

Sweden

In the Scandinavian countries, the concern with development assistance, and especially with bilateral assistance, belongs essentially to the 1960's. In 1960, the Governments of Denmark, Norway, Sweden and Finland agreed, at the recommendation of the Nordic Council, to co-ordinate their efforts in development assistance, which has resulted in joint projects of technical assistance in Korea and Tanganyika. In the early 1960's, commissions were charged with the task of reporting on the problems raised by an aid policy, and separate agencies for the management of all or part of the assistance programme had been established in Denmark, Norway and Sweden. In all countries, public opinion has, to all appearances, been favourable to an enlarged contribution to underdeveloped countries. So far, the scope and volume of Scandinavian assistance programmes remain fairly modest by international comparison, but the problems faced by Scandinavian governments are similar to those of former colonial powers turning to the larger problem of an assistance policy vis-a-vis the underdeveloped world at large. Seen in that light, the smallness of their aid programmes is not surprising.

Swedish development assistance actually began in 1952 with the formation of a private Central Committee for Swedish Technical Assistance which administered certain projects financed by public donations and government contributions. However, it was not until the 1960's that any substantial official commitments were made. First, the foreign aid policies of other countries were studied in some detail in memoranda which were published in 1962[1]. An Agency for International Assistance, charged with multilateral and bilateral technical assistance, was established at the end of 1961 and assumed the function of the Central Committee. The agency was subjected to the Ministry of Foreign Affairs; financial assistance remained in the Ministry of Finance, and budgetary appropriations were thus sought under different headings. In 1962, however, to mark the adoption of a deliberate development assistance policy, the requests were brought together in one Bill which also outlined the principles which were to guide this policy[2]. The Bill spoke of the increasing recognition of the claims of underdeveloped countries to greater economic equality; it said that:

> To the political necessity of taking account of the demands of the new nations is added the realisation of a moral obligation to help them. It is also increasingly understood that assistance offers advantages to those who help and aid seems to industrial countries an investment in future markets. Strong public opinion supports increasing assistance.

Swedish foreign aid, it continued, would not require any other motivation than the sentiment of international solidarity and responsibility. It mentioned the interest of the export industries in promoting trade with underdeveloped countries, which had been expounded with great vigour by the industrial sector[3], but took a restrictive view of development assistance:

> When assessing the economic sacrifices of advanced countries in favour of the poor countries, it is misleading to include purely commercial transactions and government measures which aim to promote their own industries in the competition for new markets (p. 7).

A preference was expressed for multilateral assistance, but not to the exclusion of bilateral assistance, for which three motives were given. Certain tasks, such as family planning, were inadequately attended to in multilateral technical assistance and seemed appropriate for Swedish contributions. Secondly, bilateral contacts with receiving countries might stimulate greater personal effort within the framework of technical assistance programmes. Finally, it was argued that:

> The fact that most countries give their aid in this form makes it necessary for us to do so if our assistance is to be increased significantly ;

---

1. *Aspekter på utvecklingsbiståndet.* Statens offentliga utredningar 1962 : 12 (Stockholm, 1962).
2. *Kungl. Maj:ts proposition nr 100 år, 1962* (Government Bill No. 100, 1962).
3. E.g. in SNS. *The Swedish Economy and the Underdeveloped Countries* (Stockholm, 1961).

otherwise, Sweden would become far too prominent in multilateral programmes (p. 19).

Technical assistance was regarded as particularly valuable, and the government took the position that technical assistance, multilateral and bilateral, should be given priority in Swedish aid programmes. At the same time, it was anticipated that the shortage of suitable personnel would set limits to the rapid expansion of technical assistance and that an increase in total Swedish aid would therefore entail an increasing volume of financial assistance. It was stated that such assistance ought to take the form of loans, as this would "underline the fact that it is a profitable economic transaction between equal partners" (p. 17). Terms were to be set in accordance with balance of payments conditions and ability to pay, and in the case of social projects, pure grants might be justified.

In accordance with this policy declaration, appropriations for Swedish assistance have been increased at a rapid pace in recent years. The administration of the expanding Agency for International Assistance gave rise to sharp criticism and was subjected to review and reorganisation in 1963, 1964, and 1965 resulting eventually in the transfer of financial assistance to the aid agency.

Bilateral financial aid was started in the form of paper gifts for educational purposes to a number of Asian countries, and a few development loans have been granted. Thus, in the autumn of 1964, an agreement with India provided for a grant covering among other things continued paper shipments and untied 20-year loans at 2 per cent have been accorded to a number of countries, some in the framework of international consortia. An increasing interest in aid linked to Swedish exports has been expressed.

Multilateral contributions have been increased by voluntary increases in the Swedish contribution to the IDA. All in all, the Swedish aid programme has increased considerably in scope in recent years; limiting factors have probably been the difficulty of rapidly establishing suitable administrative machinery and of defining a policy of bilateral financial aid.

Norway

In Norway, as in the other Scandinavian countries, the aid programme is generally considered as a humanitarian enterprise and a contribution to international solidarity. There has been little interest in linking the aid programme to the promotion of Norwegian exports. Although the aid programme seems to enjoy both public and parliamentary support, it remains modest by any and all standards of international comparison.

In 1960, a commission was appointed to investigate the problem of Norwegian assistance and, in 1962, the Norwegian Agency for International Development, operating under the Foreign Office, was created to administer the entire aid programme. For the beginning, multilateral contributions, especially to the United Nations' EPTA and Special Fund, to IBRD, and lately IDA, have dominated the aid effort. The bilateral programme has so far taken the form almost exclusively of technical assistance projects, although one loan has been made to Turkey within the Turkish Consortium. However, it is now the declared policy to increase bilateral aid, although this has so far run into administrative bottlenecks and a shortage of projects.

The most unusual feature of Norwegian foreign aid is perhaps the direct tax of one-quarter of 1 per cent on personal income, earmarked for development aid, which was introduced in 1964 and which, according to recent suggestions, may be increased in the future.

The technical assistance programme is concentrated in India, Korea (in connection with a Nordic project), and in East Africa; historical accident seems in great measure to have dictated these choices. A Peace Corps programme was initiated in 1963 and, by the end of 1964, involved some 60 volunteers serving in Uganda.

Although Norwegian authorities find the search for bilateral projects frustrating, the various consortia within which bilateral contributions could be "multilateralised" have not had much appeal, possibly because they do not supply that measure of identification which is everywhere a powerful impulse behind bilateral aid giving.

Denmark

Broadly speaking, the situation in Denmark appears quite similar, although the Danish aid programme is even more modest. There is no explicit aid opposition. In the political debate and editoria comments, an increased aid programme is generally considered desirable, although the public opinion poll cited in Chapter III suggests that the aid issue may raise less enthusiasm than the debate on public platforms would indicate. The bulk of the assistance programme consists of contributions to multilateral agencies, but after 1962 when an agency was created to be charged with the execution of the assistance programme, the intention has been to expand bilateral assistance. Financial aid of a bilateral character has, however, been limited, and the funds appropriated by the Folketing have been committed and dispersed very slowly, owing to the difficulty of finding and negotiating suitable projects. So far, loans have been made to India, Tunisia and to Turkey in the OECD Consortium. Denmark has also become a member of the Greek Consortium. The terms of the Indian loan are of some interest: it is a ten-year loan at 5 per cent rate of interest, but repayments are to be made in rupees and extended as technical assistance grants. This formula has not, however, been followed in the later loans. All have been tied to procurement in Denmark.

Technical assistance projects have thus dominated the bilateral programme. Unlike most donors of bilateral aid, especially small ones, Denmark did not at first concentrate such activities in a few receiving countries, but chose to begin a large number of small projects spread out over many developing countries in the hope of gaining wider experience. In 1964, two years after the beginning of the programme, Danish bilateral projects had thus been negotiated or planned in more than 30 developing countries[1]. By that time, it was decided for administrative reasons to concentrate future assistance on a narrow choice of countries and already a large team of medical experts in Congo (Leopoldville), and a group of volunteers in Tanzania, dominated the programme.

---

1. P. Nyboe Andersen, "Denmark's Aid to the Developing Countries", *Danish Foreign Office Journal*, No. 49, June, 1964, p. 26.

CANADA

The Canadian aid programme is strongly coloured by Canada's membership in the Commonwealth. After the end of the war, Canada extended much assistance to the United Kingdom and other NATO members and since 1950 she has been a member of the Colombo plan under which more than 80 per cent of her contributions to economic aid programmes since then have been appropriated. Various Commonwealth programmes account for much of the remaining bilateral aid[1].

In recent years an effort has been made to pull together the elements of the Canadian aid system and, in 1960, an External Aid Office was set up under the Minister of External Affairs. A policy-making board includes representatives of the Ministries of Finance, External Affairs, and Trade and Commerce, and of the Bank of Canada. Export credits, on the other hand, which since 1961 have been made available for exports of capital goods (with payment periods over five years), remain separately administered.

As it has emerged gradually, the Canadian aid programme has not been endowed with an explicit doctrine. Strategic motives and considerations of national security have been of little account. Until recently, Canadian aid was largely in the form of grants and it has been suggested that the predominantly humanitarian motives for Canadian aid were expressed both in this fact and in the relatively modest proportions of Canadian aid[2]. Lately, however, new programmes have been initiated both for long-term export financing at 6 per cent and for very long development loans on so-called IDA terms with 50 years maturity, 10 years grade period and 0.75 per cent service charges. An unusual and novel feature of the Canadian aid system is an agreement with the Inter-American Development Bank which is to administer $10 million of such soft loans in Latin American countries, selecting and approving suitable projects.

JAPAN

Foreign aid to underdeveloped countries has been part of the official policy of Japan since the mid-1950's, and Japan was one of the original members of the Development Assistance Group and later of DAC, although she became a full member of OECD only in 1964. The flow of financial resources from Japan to underdeveloped countries is of considerable magnitude and places her in the fifth place among OECD providers of development finance.

Grants accounted for a fairly large share of the Japanese bilateral flow in the early years, but it should be remembered that most of these grants constituted of payments under reparations agreements with Burma, the Philippines, Indonesia and Vietnam[3]. While these payments, which are tide to Japanese goods and services, may serve purposes similar to other types of development assistance and be administered in similar ways, it is obviously relevant to a study of the sources of aid policy to remember their character.

---

1. Irving Brecher, "Canada's Foreign Economic Aid", *The Canadian Banker*, Vol. LXIX (Winter, 1962).
2. Brecher, *op. cit.*
3. For the commitments under reparations agreements, see John White, *Japanese Aid* (London, 1964), p. 53.

Similarly, Japanese lending remains almost exclusively in the form of credits from the Export-Import Bank, which was established already in 1950 to serve "the purpose of facilitating through financial aid Japan's economic interchange, mainly in the field of trade, with foreign countries"[1]. Under this operation, which antedates the official adoption of a development assistance policy, loans to foreign borrowers are extended on hard terms. In spite of a certain reduction of interest rates in recent years, the average rate is close to 6 per cent, and maturities closer to 10 than to 20 years. Such loans are largely tied to Japanese exports and extended on application from Japanese exporters and commercial banks, and in principle only if financing is not available from other sources although the project is sound.

Only a smaller part of financial aid has been extended directly to foreign governments in the form of so-called "yen credits", mostly through the consortia for India and Pakistan.

The Overseas Economic Co-operation Fund, which was set up in 1961 specifically to provide loans on softer terms to less developed countries, has until now been active only on a limited scale. Technical assistance through the Overseas Technical Co-operation Agency, created in 1962, is in the budget included under the same heading as export promotion.

To facilitate Japan's "economic interchange" with foreign countries was long an avowed and obvious purpose of Japanese activities in development finance, but in official pronouncements the diplomatic aspects of assistance, especially to neighbouring Asian countries, has been given increasing emphasis in recent years. The Prime Minister, speaking in the Japanese Diet on October 18, 1963, said:

> It is quite natural that Japan should extend assistance to other countries as she herself has attained such remarkable economic growth, and Japan must also make a greater effort to establish friendly relations of solidarity with Asian countries, bearing in mind the necessity for stability and peace in all of Asia[2].

While recognising the responsibility to contribute to the less developed countries, Japanese declarations at home and in international organisations reply to criticism of the commercial character and hard terms of her lending to developing countries by pointing to the difficulties of maintaining her own high rate of growth and the strain on her balance of payments.

Detailed public discussion of aid policy seems, however, to have been negligible until the publication by the Ministry for International Trade and Industry (Miti) in 1963 of a report on *The Present Status and Programmes of Economic Co-operation*[3]. This report presented an extensive description of development assistance programmes and volume in Japan and other countries and proposed a rapid stepping-up of Japanese aid, the promotion of private investment, wider Japanese participation in international consortia and other forms of international co-ordination of aid, an increase in development loans to foreign governments on soft terms, and more technical assistance. The Foreign Ministry showed itself unenthusiastic and in the ensuing press discussion demands for improved co-ordination and adminis-

---

1. Article 1, Export-Import Bank Law.
2. *Waga Gaiko no Kinkyo* (Tokyo, 1964) (Blue Book on *Recent Japanese Foreign Policy*, Vol. 8).
3. *Keizai-Kyoryoku no Guenjo to Mondaiten*.

tration were made, similar to those periodically raised in all countries with development assistance policies[1]. In Japan, the Ministries of Foreign Affairs, Finance, and International Trade and Industry, as well as the Economic Planning Agency, are charged with different parts of the system of foreign aid and finance. This administrative structure in some measure reflects the character of the Japanese system — its roots, not in colonial policy, but in the problem posed by the transfer of reparations and in a policy of export promotion. The recognition of "foreign aid to underdeveloped countries" as a political, economic, and statistical concept, has been gradual and, as in many other countries, largely the result of the influence of the international aid system.

The European Economic Community

Although it may for many purposes be termed a multilateral operation, the development assistance administered by the European Economic Community also has many of the characteristics of a bilateral aid programme.

From the very beginning of the negotiations leading to the Treaty of Rome, the French government insisted that the participating states should jointly engage in development assistance to colonies and other dependent territories. At the ministerial meeting at Messina in 1955, the creation of an investment fund for this purpose was inscribed on the agenda for immediate study. In an annex to the Treaty of 1957 provision was later made for a Development Fund for Overseas Countries and Territories to finance welfare and infrastructure projects on a grant basis. After the accession to independence of most of the colonies, a new convention of association was negotiated, signed in 1963, and providing in the area of development assistance for continued grants-in-aid as well as for soft development loans and hard loans on conventional terms. Subscriptions to the fund are distributed by quotas among the members, with one-third each from Germany and France, somewhat more than 10 per cent from Italy, and slightly less than 10 per cent from Belgium and Holland each.

Especially in Germany and the Netherlands, this contribution to an aid programme for French and Belgian ex-colonies in Africa has been criticised as inconsistent with both the economic and political assumptions underlying aid policies in those countries. For the Community as such, however, this policy, in combination with the other measures of integration linking the African associated states to the Common Market, amounts to the adoption of a "special relationship" with these African countries, and although an extension of the Community's foreign aid to other developing nations in other parts of the world is frequently discussed, the links between Europe and Africa have come to be seen as especially close. In the words of Professor Hallstein :

> The economic, geographic, and historical ties between Europe and Africa confer upon the Community an indispensable part in the development of the African continent from which it cannot and will not shrink[2].

---

1. For one impression of the reception of the Miti Report, see White, *Japanese Aid*, p. 30.
2. Speech at the Eleventh Joint Meeting of the Consultative Assembly of Europe and the European Parliament at Strasbourg, June 12, 1964.

Development Assistance from the Soviet Bloc

Although Soviet economic assistance falls outside the scope of this report, a few words about it are warranted by its obvious political importance in the system of "competitive coexistence".

Such assistance to the developing countries outside the Soviet bloc started in 1954. The Stalinist policy of economic isolation had not left room for foreign economic relations outside the bloc. Foreign policy with respect to developing countries had been confined to the traditional struggle against colonialism. This policy was gradually replaced, as the colonies became independent, by the approach know as "peaceful coexistence", which enabled the Soviets to abandon obsolete issues. Anti-colonialism became irrelevant, and to accuse the leaders of the new nations of being "imperialist lackeys" soon proved unprofitable. Western countries, especially the United States, were making rapid progress in strengthening political and, often, military relationships with the newly independent countries by means of economic assistance programmes, and it became increasingly clear that the Soviet bloc could not persist in its aloofness. Moreover, a modest foreign assistance programme appeared to be feasible without causing an undue drain on the Soviet economy.

Political ideology had to be adapted, however, in order to make possible the co-operation of the bloc with the "bourgeois" governments of developing countries, as well as the co-operation between local communist movements and democratic parties. An intensive campaign started against "sectarian narrowness", which compelled local communists to make a common cause with the nationalist groups against imperialism and neo-colonialism. This tactical manoeuvre did not find support in all communist countries, especially not in Red China, but it enabled Soviet leaders to start a pragmatic programme of economic co-operation with developing non-Communist countries, unhampered by ideological restrictions.

The objectives of the Soviet assistance programme have never been clearly stated by Soviet leaders, and any assessments in this respect must be tentative. Obviously, political considerations play an important role in bloc assistance. The belief in the world triumph of communism is still one of the guiding grinciples of USSR policy, and there is no reason to assume that the economic offensive in developing countries ultimately is meant to serve another purpose. In the view of Soviet leaders, economic development is closely connected to industrialisation and urbanisation, which has been the historic prerequisite for a powerful communist movement. Moreover, the Soviets probably do not seriously believe rapid economic development to be possible without using totalitarian methods; developing countries can thus be expected to have to apply Soviet methods of development when achievements along democratic lines lag behind expectations.

Apart from these long run political objectives, some economic motivation is conceivable. It has been claimed, for instance, that the imports of raw materials from the developing countries on the basis of long term barter agreements are seen as a welcome aspect of foreign assistance[1]. It is also officially stated that the Soviet assistance programme is based on mutual

---

1. Klaus Billerbeck, *Die Auslandshilfe des Ostblocks für die Entwicklungsländer* (Hamburg, 1960).

economic benefit of both the Soviet bloc and the developing countries. The propagandistic aspect of such a pronouncement is evident, but the terms of Soviet assistance confirm this "businesslike" statement.

In comparison to Western assistance programmes, the Soviet programme is extremely small. It consists almost exclusively of loans on rather soft terms, with interest rates varying usually from 2 to $2\frac{1}{2}$ per cent, and maturities of 12 years. Chinese aid, however, has been given in the form of very long interest-free loans. In the following table, commitments and disbursements are given for the Sino-Soviet bloc as a whole between 1954 and 1963. It has been estimated that the assistance from Communist China was about 10 per cent of the cumulative total by 1963, but this share is probably rising. A relatively large share of 20/25 per cent has been contributed by the Eastern European bloc countries.

ECONOMIC ASSISTANCE[1] OF THE SINO-SOVIET BLOC
TO DEVELOPING COUNTRIES, 1954-1963

Millions of Dollars.

Year	Commitments	Disbursements
1954	11	1
1955	149	3
1956	608	107
1957	227	87
1958	556	205
1959	894	161
1960	1,165	186
1961	957	294
1962	507	391
1963	319	(425)
Cumulative total 1954 to 1963	5,393	1.860

1. Excluding military assistance.
Source : OECD statistics.

As can be seen, commitments rose until 1960, then flattened off. The sharp drop in 1962 is probably due to the considerable amount of commitments that had not been utilised by that date (75 per cent). Already much earlier, Berliner, writing about the sharp rise in commitments in 1957, argued that it was quite possible that the Soviets were not aiming at "an endless progression, but rather a quick building up to a certain plateau and a levelling off after that"[1].

If the Soviet bloc assistance programme is compared to the programme of the OECD countries combined, it is small even in nominal value (4.7 per cent of the flow of official resources from OECD countries in 1963). If a crude attempt is made to estimate the "real value" of the burden of development loans by estimating the discounted present value of future repayments (see Chapter IV), the Soviet programme appears as roughly 1 per cent of the total OECD programme. In spite of this, the political impact of Soviet aid has undoubtedly been considerable. Several factors have apparently

---

1. Joseph S. Berliner, *Soviet Economic Aid, The New Aid and Trade Policy in Underdeveloped Countries*, New York, 1958, p. 188.

contributed to this success, and the terms and the forms of assistance seem to be most important.

As already said, the terms of Soviet loans have usually been soft, though there are exceptions, especially in the case of smaller loans extended by the European satellites. Soviet loans are repayable in local currency or in commodities, and Soviet assistance is closely linked to trade. From the balance of payments point of view, this aspect is highly attractive to both parties. Instead of buying raw materials on European markets with valuable foreign exchange, the Soviet bloc can deal directly with the primary producing countries. The LDC's import equipment from the bloc countries and avoid the foreign exchange difficulties they face with Western economies. Though the absorptive capacity for raw materials in the Soviet bloc is limited, this feature of Soviet assistance has been attractive to developing countries, while the fluctuating prices on world markets are viewed with considerable dismay. The prices and conditions offered by the Soviet bloc have not always been favourable, but there is reason to assume that the Soviets will try to avoid these mistakes in the future.

The Soviet assistance effort is generally regarded as superior in its timing. The Soviet Union has often been able to play the role of "buyer of last resort" in emergencies when world markets have failed or political developments have caused serious difficulties (Cuban sugar, for instance). These actions have created the impression of concealed economic assistance, although they were essentially trade transactions.

The forms of bloc assistance nevertheless confirm the impression that the Soviets are genuinely aiming to promote development in the developing countries, as most students of Soviet aid agree. Contrary to a widespread impression, Soviet assistance does not mainly take the form of "impact aid" without much of a contribution to economic development[1]. An important part of bloc assistance is earmarked for specific projets of obvious development value. Only 5 per cent of the assistance programme is non-project assistance and mainly meant to pay for services like technical assistance. More than half of the total (53 per cent) is derected to industrial projects, but energy, irrigation, transportation, and communication also loom large.

Soviet assistance is heavily concentrated. Four countries, India, the United Arabic Republic, Afghanistan and Brazil, have accounted for about half of the cumulative total of commitments up to and including 1963. For the year 1963, Algeria alone accounted for half of the total commitments. From the geographic distribution, it is clear that Soviet aid is largely given to developing countries that manifest their strong opposition to military alignment with Western countries.

CONCLUSION

What even this cursory survey of the aid systems of the major countries demonstrates is the heterogeneity both of actual aid policies and of the motives behind them. It should not be forgotten that, regardless of the motives and direction of their aid policies, countries engaging in development assistance will often encounter the same practical problems and that the examination and mutual review of bilateral aid policies in DAC and elsewhere

---

1. See, for instance, Berliner, *op. cit.*, p. 22.

has created, at the very least, a shared language and a conceptual framework, and possibly the beginnings of a code of good behaviour. But when one focuses on the differences, it appears that, rather than one system of direct development assistance, there are at least four distinct ones:

i) The United States involvement with the developing countries chiefly reflects a concern with world-wide political development both in its long run aspects. Such a broad view of the role of development assistance is not taken explicitly in other donor countries. United States aid in many countries is so extensive as to inevitably make the donor intimately concerned with development strategy as a whole, and it is increasingly administered on the criterion of efficiency in overall development performance.

ii) The former colonial powers play a similar role in some of their old possessions, notably in Africa, but are groping towards modes of marginal assistance to other areas, partly in response to international efforts to co-ordinate bilateral assistance through consortia and partly to extend the use of development assistance as economic diplomacy.

iii) A third group of countries, notably Germany and Japan, have made extensive grants and loans throughout the underdeveloped world, characteristically in the form of specific projects, rather than general support of development plans, and aiming frankly at promoting the economic relationship between donor and recipient.

iv) Smaller donor countries have generally shied away from extensive financial assistance on a bilateral basis, in some cases with the explicit motivation that they would be unable to support many countries on any significant scale and have no reason to favour one rather than another. They therefore concentrate on technical assistance and participate in international consortia, but reserve most of their strictly financial support for multilateral contributions.

As the motives and the relationship between individual donors and recipient countries inevitably vary, so then do the forms of aid. The discussion about such technical aspects of development assistance as the choice between project and programme assistance, loans and grants, tied and untied aid, is incomplete unless it is realised to what an extent these choices will tend to be influenced by specific and individual circumstances rather than by an abstract conception of development assistance. Some of these issues will be considered in Chapter V.

III

PUBLIC OPINION ON FOREIGN AID

It is often said that in the major donor countries public opinion is hostile, guarded, or indifferent to the foreign aid issue. On the other hand, it is asserted that, in the smaller countries — whose contributions are small even relative to their size and income — public opinion is favourable to a larger effort.

Such impressions usually derive from the debate in the press, pronouncements by political leaders, or editorial statements. The public in the first group of countries is described as increasingly impatient with the "lack of results" and with the prospect of a permanent aid programme; accounts of waste or of profligate spending and corruption by politicians in underdeveloped countries are said to be given wider attention than successful development projects, and political crises or hostile positions on the part of recipient countries are said to dismay the public.

In the second group of countries, opinion is thought to be critical of the commercial and political overtones in much bilateral aid, and anxious to extend some sort of disinterested assistance, largely multilateral, and to increase the sacrifice beyond that currently imposed by their governments.

Actually, of course, attitudes towards foreign aid policies will not, in a democracy, be uniform. Particularly when the issue is not an extreme choice between some foreign aid and none, but rather how much and in what forms foreign aid should be extended, opinion is bound, as in all matters of public finance, to be divided — when not indifferent. Undoubtedly, acute observers of the political scene may at times form a valid impression of the predominant mood in political circles, perhaps even in the electorate as a whole. But, whether the debate about foreign aid is relatively heated, as in the United States, or thin, as in most other countries, it is difficult to do more than speculate about the state of public opinion merely on the basis of public statements, not only when they are contradictory but also when such pronouncements happen to be unanimously positive.

Genuine studies of public attitudes in this field are rare, and no comparative research has been done. Public attitudes towards any government spending programme are often difficult to summarise neatly. What one student has called the "lack of congruence in people's thinking about fiscal programs" may thus produce strong support for some kind of government spending as long as the question of its financing is not raised, but firm opposition to the thought of raising taxes for the same purpose[1]. Experience gained

---

1. Eva Mueller, "Public Attitudes Toward Fiscal Programs", *Quarterly Journal of Economics*, Vol. LXXVII (May 1963), p. 222.

from studies of attitudes to foreign aid also suggests that they are unstable for many other reasons as well, so that answers to pollsters depend very much on the formulation and the context of the questions posed. Finally a distinction ought undoubtedly to be made between attitudes of the public at large and "effective opinion" which on this, as on many other issues, is made and held by relatively small groups.

Many of the difficulties in talking about opinions and attitudes on the subject of foreign aid are amply illustrated in Dieter Danckwortt's study of German attitudes toward development aid and underdeveloped countries[1]. Based in part on interviews with sample groups ranging from politicians to the girl-friends of foreign trainees, and in part on a content analysis of 1500 publications appearing between 1950 and 1959, Danckwortt's survey stresses the complexity and diversity of the problem, and this alone puts it in a different category from conventional polls.

Even among parliamentarians and civil servants, who were well informed about the German aid programme, attitudes were various and sometimes conflicting. While many younger politicians seemed to have an unproblematic sense of solidarity with developing countries, older ones were more cautious; travel and experience of conditions in underdeveloped countries was closely correlated with a positive interest in development aid[2]. In the civil service, views and doctrines were not the same in different departments and ranks. Diplomatic officials laid stress on political aspects of the aid relationship; economists were concerned with the world economy and inclined to resent political complications. Top officials were exhilarated by the pioneering nature of their task and the novelty of international co-operation, while their subordinates in charge of administrative execution often complained of overwork, frustration, and confusion. Conflict tended to arise in the co-operation between officials with long and traditional civil service background and younger academics drawn into the new tasks of development assistance, and the public and the business sector were sometimes felt to be indifferent and too self-interested.

In the business world and among trade union officials, there was greater stress on anti-communism, and among workers in contact with foreign trainees on the job, a diffuse fear of the explosiveness of the underdeveloped world and a sense of superiority and criticism of lack of discipline, order, and punctuality. Landladies of foreign trainees had no associations to the concept of underdeveloped countries but were concerned with the cleanliness of their tenants; like most other non-professional groups, they had no special feeling of obligation toward developing countries.

The content analysis revealed practically no argument for aid that was not contradicted by another, and the ambivalence and confusion seemed to give rise to the frequent calls for a "new conception" of foreign aid[3]. Ethical and humanitarian motives were stressed by many writers, questioned by others who urged a tougher approach. While anti-Communism was frequently cited, there was little belief in the efficacy of aid as a political instrument and also the view that Germany's lack of political ambitious would strengthen

---

1. Dieter Danckwortt, *Zur Psychologie der deutschen Entwicklungshilfe* (Baden-Baden and Bonn, 1962).
2. *Ibid.*, p. 45.
3. *Ibid.*, p. 82.

the developing countries' confidence in her. Some writers stressed the idealistic and political value of an aid policy for Germany self.

Economic motives were at times regarded as cleaner and more honest than political ones which were assumed to be sordid and self-interested, but other writers complained about the confusion of economic and ethical motives and asked that aid should be clearly distinguished from export promotion. Sometimes it was stressed that aid required a sacrifice, but even in the same document it might be argued that aid would also bring economic gain to all parties.

There was much self-criticism of the superficiality of German attitudes and objectives, much spontaneous hope for sympathy, gratitude and admiration, and much warning against any such self-deception. On the emotional level, the diffuse threat posed by the problem of the underdeveloped countries seemed to cause vague anxiety, but sometimes foreign aid also seemed to inspire feelings of superiority, not only vis-à-vis underdeveloped countries, but vis-à-vis other aid donors, notably the colonial powers and the United States, whose past and present mistakes caused a certain glee. However, German aid and especially technical assistance programmes were also subjected to a barrage of criticism on all counts. Programmes for foreign trainees were attacked for their methods of selection, briefing procedures, the inadequacies of the reception and the consequent maladjustment of the trainees.

Although no similar study seems to have been made in any other country, even a cursory familiarity with press comment on aid policies in other donor countries suggests that similar ambivalence and confusion is widely spread. This does not necessarily weaken the general support of an aid policy: indeed, in a study of French opinion on foreign aid it has been suggested that one reason for the favourable position taken by the French public was the very complexity of the foreign aid issue which made it possible for different groups to lend it a meaning that suited them. In the words of the Institut Français de l'Opinion Publique "its intellectual image is imprecise and multivalent while its affective meaning is strong and compelling".

There have been two highly interesting and intensive studies of French attitudes to foreign assistance, both undertaken on behalf of the Ministry of Co-operation. The first concerned only attitudes to the policy of assistance to French-speaking Africa, as of late 1962 — which, however, comprised virtually the entire aid policy at the time — but the second poll, which was taken in September, 1964, was extended to cover attitudes toward aid to underdeveloped countries in general[1].

The first of these studies showed that attitudes towards foreign aid reflected a good deal of tension and uncertainty and consequently were quite unstable. Thus, to an isolated question whether France should help French-speaking African countries, only 41 per cent answered "yes" and 37 per cent

---

1. Ministère de la Coopération, *10 Réponses sur l'Afrique. Opinions sur la Coopération entre l'Afrique et la France* (Paris, 1963). This published report was based largely on the poll and analysis by the Institut Français de l'Opinion Publique : *La Coopération entre la France et les Etats Africains et Malgaches. Opinions et Attitudes des Français. Octobre-décembre, 1962.* The results of the second poll were presented in *Attitudes des Français vis-à-vis des Problèmes de Coopération, septembre 1964.* These two unpublished reports were made available through the courtesy of IFOP and the Ministère de la Coopération.

said "no". When the same question was put in the context of a major inquiry into attitudes towards the African states and the policy of co-operation, the percentage answering "yes" rose to 73 per cent, and only 13 per cent said "no". In an elite group described as *"cadres"* and characterised by high education and responsible positions, the percentage in favour was 88 per cent, those opposed only 7 per cent.

Behind this strong support of an aid policy were found a great variety of attitudes : when asked to choose the weightiest from a list of arguments in favour of aid to French-speaking Africa, the answers suggested that "the majority of Frenchmen retain an attitude towards African countries which is very marked by colonialism[1]".

The principal choices were:

They helped us during the war, we cannot drop them now	34%
Aid guarantees us outlets for our products and sources of supply of raw materials	28%
Aid is the best means of preserving our cultural influence	23%
There must be solidarity between the rich countries and the developing countries	20%
We cannot abandon them now that we have started them in their development	20%

However, these figures conceal significant differences among social groups. The first argument carried distinctly more weight among farmers, groups of lower education, and lower income brackets. The second, economic, argument seemed to have roughly the same appeal in most groups, but the stresse on cultural influence in the third proposition was the most popular among the highly educated, the professional groups, and higher income brackets. These groups were generally more favourable to the principle of foreign aid: among those with higher education, 91 per cent were in favour of aid.

Although a majoriy supported the aid policy, 58 per cent approved of critical arguments. Thus, four out of ten agreed that "we have enough to do in our own underdeveloped regions". This argument, however, seemed to be invoked to limit aid rather than refuse it entirely; 61 per cent of those citing it were nevertheless favourable to aid in general; on the other hand, 60 per cent of those who thought aid expenditures excessive approved the proposition. Only relatively few were inclined to accept other criticisms as important: that the aid "benefits an inefficient elite" (18 per cent), that the recipients were "incapable of utilising our aid well" (15 per cent), that they were "too ungrateful" (11 per cent).

Questions concerning the magnitude of French aid to ex-colonial Africa met with a high percentage of "don't-knows". As many as 28 per cent had no opinion on whether the current aid effort was warranted; 37 per cent approved of it, while 23 per cent found it excessive and 12 per cent inadequate. These ratios were strongly dependent on economic and social factors: thus, in the 18-24 age bracket, 25 per cent thought the aid effort too small, while among those over 65, only 7 per cent thought so. Tradesmen and farmers were more anxious to reduce aid than employees and workers and, when the question was broadened to cover the desirability of an increase

---

1. Ministère de la Coopération, *10 Réponses...*, p. 30.

in aid even if each tax payer would have to contribute more, they were the least enthusiastic. Of the general population, 17 per cent were in favour of such increased contributions, but 69 per cent were opposed. Among the most highly educated, the percentage in favour rose to 32 per cent; among those with elementary education, it was 13 per cent.

As to the forms of aid, there seemed to be a widespread opinion that technical and cultural assistance were the most desirable. Financial assistance was viewed with rather less favour. In a previous enquiry in 1960, Frenchmen were asked whether they approved of financial aid to colonies becoming independent : 36 per cent were then opposed and only 29 per cent in favour. In 1962, they were asked to choose the two most desirable forms of aid out of a list of seven : 45 per cent cited technical assistance, 43 per cent cultural aid, 23 per cent financial aid.

Two-thirds of all respondents preferred to see French aid dispensed by France herself, and this attitude was more pronounced among the "cadres". Fourteen per cent favoured multilateral aid through an international organisation and of these 7 per cent mentioned the European Economic Community, 5 per cent the United Nations.

The study made an attempt to probe racial attitudes by means of depth interviews of a subsample, and it was possible to show a strong relationship between racial views and attitudes towards aid policies. Negative attitudes to negroes, which, in France, as elsewhere, are correlated with lack of education and information, were strongly associated with negative views on aid, its good uses, and the wisdom of continuing it. But an ambivalent attitude towards Africans was widespread even among those who strongly favoured aid. Indeed, it seems likely that a good deal of the affect in attitudes on the aid issue stems from internal conflict and the desire to suppress racist impulses.

Broadly speaking, the poll of 1964 confirmed that aid policy was seen favourably by a majority of Frenchmen, and on many issues views appeared slightly more uniform than two years earlier. Among the indisputable shifts in opinion was a reversal of the priorities accorded to aid to North Africa and sub-Saharan Africa : in 1962 almost half of the respondents placed North Africa in the first rank and 23 per cent the French-speaking countries of Africa South of the Sahara ; in 1964, 51 per cent of those interviewed placed the latter countries first and only 15 per cent gave first priority to North Africa.

Among motives cited for aiding underdeveloped countries, human solidarity and justice were cited by the largest number, the fight against hunger and underdevelopment was next, and the promotion of French interests was mentioned by less than 20 per cent. (The desire to forestall the growth of communism was cited by only 1 per cent.) As for the objectives of aid to French-speaking and sub-Saharan Africa, most respondents, faced with a list of four, chose the promotion of these countries' ability to develop (36 per cent), 21 per cent the maintenance of favourable economic relations, 16 per cent the maintenance of French influence, and only 12 per cent the "rayonnement" of French language and civilisation.

Cruder public opinion polls are available for a number of countries, but in contemplating such percentages of favourable and unfavourable answers, it is undoubtedly wise to bear in mind how complex the underlying motives and arguments are likely to be.

In the *United States,* Gallup polls which are often quoted have shown a substantial majority of positive replies to the plain question : "In general, how do you feel about foreign aid — are you for it, or against it ?" In 1963, answers were even slightly more positive than in 1958 :[1]

In percentage.

	1958	1963
For	51	58
Against	33	30
No Opinion	16	12

This corresponds roughly with the results of a set of re-interviews with identical respondents in a study of attitudes before the elections of 1956 and 1960[2]. Asked whether "the United States should give economic help to poorer countries, even if those countries can't pay for it" *(sic),* 44 per cent of the respondents agreed and 15 per cent disagreed in 1956, while in 1960 52 per cent agreed and 19 per cent disagreed :

In percentage.

	1956	1960
Agree strongly	21	29
Agree, but not strongly	22	23
Not sure, depends	32	28
Disagree, but not strongly	10	6
Disagree strongly	15	13

On the other hand, when asked, in 1961, whether the government should spend more, less, or the same on a number of programmes, not many respondents favoured an expansion of foreign aid. In a long list of programmes of public spending, "help to other countries" fared distinctly worse than any other, as illustrated by a few excerpts[3] :

Government should spend...

In percentage.

	More	Less	Same	No opinion	More, even if taxes had to be raised
Help for older people	70	3	23	4	34
Education	60	7	25	8	41
Defence rearmament	47	6	34	13	30
Space exploration	26	32	28	14	14
Help to other countries	7	53	28	12	2

1. Cf. Coffin, *Witness for Aid*, p. 37.
2. Campbell, Converse, Miller and Stokes, *The American Voter*, (New York, 1960), cited in Mueller, "Public Attitudes...", p. 226.
3. Mueller, "Public Attitudes...", p. 215.

This negative attitude towards increased foreign aid spending was at least in 1961 even more pronounced in higher income groups than in lower. Index values (per cent advocating increased spending, minus per cent advocating decreased spending) of attitudes towards these programmes were as follows[1]:

Family income.

	UNDER $3,000	$3,000–$7,500	$7,500 AND OVER
Help for older people	68	67	64
Education	43	59	53
Defence, rearmament	35	42	45
Space exploration	—18	—2	5
Help to other countries	—38	—46	—51

These polls seems to show that, although in the United States a policy of *some* foreign assistance finds support in public opinion, it does not rank highly in the public's preferences for alternative types of public spending.

In *Germany*, a number of different polls have been taken, which seem to indicate a substantial majority in favour of aid, although the trend in the 1960's seems to have been against it. One report concerns answers given in 1963 to the question: "Do you find it right or wrong that the Bundesrepublik participates in the industrial countries' effort to help the developing countries in Asia, Africa, and Latin America?"[2] To this question, 46 per cent replied in favour and 38 per cent were opposed. The occupational groups most favourable were civil servants, then followed private white-collar employees, professionals, workers and, eventually, farmers. Humanitarian motives were cited four times as often as political ones, with economic reasons in between. The younger age groups were more favourable, and those with higher education approved of the aid policy almost twice as often as those with merely primary education.

In 1959 and 1960, a large part of the German public was still unaware of the existence of German development assistance. In October, 1959, 38 per cent responded to one question on this subject that they did not know wether or not Germany aided underdeveloped countries. As the question was repeated at different times, this group declined, but so did the number of those in favour of such aid. The question: "Are you for or against our giving financial aid to the underdeveloped countries in Africa and Asia?" received the following answers[3]:

In percentage.

	1959 OCT.	1960 JULY	1962 JUNE	1963 JULY	1963 NOV.
For	62	64	46	51	47
Against	17	15	29	25	27
Undecided	13	11	15	16	18
No Opinion	8	10	10	8	8

1. *Ibid.*, p. 230.
2. The only published report seems to be brief account given by Herr Scheel before the International Public Relations Association in Berlin on 30th May, 1963. Reprinted in *Handbuch der Entwicklungshilfe*, II A 30, p. 191 ff.
3. By courtesy of Institut für Demoskopie, Allensbach.

The Scandinavian countries are among those where public opinion has been thought to be particularly positive to aid policy, but a series of Gallup polls from *Denmark* suggest that there, as elsewhere, opinion is divided. The question posed by the Danish Gallup Institute was, however, not whether Denmark should or should not give *some* foreign aid, but whether Denmark should give one per cent of its national income to underdeveloped countries. The answers to this question were[1]:

In percentage.

	1960	1962	1965
For	48	36	40
Against	14	35	30
Don't know	38	29	30

These figures point if anything to an increasing reluctance to consider committing large resources to foreign aid. The stand for such aid was in half the cases motivated by reference to political urgency; the negative position by reference to lack of resources, the need to develop Greenland, and the waste of aid in underdeveloped countries.

In *Canada,* a study reportedly undertaken by the Canadian Peace Research Institute, has found support of foreign aid considerably weaker in the public than among politicians[2]. While 73 per cent of a sample of political leaders from all parties proclaimed themselves in favour of increasing foreign aid, only 12 per cent of the public took this position, and twice as many would like to see it reduced.

Although, as already said, there are no comparative studies of attitudes to foreign aid, a study of public opinion in the European Economic Community included two questions with a bearing on the problem[3]. In the various member countries, respondents were asked whether they were for or against the use of tax revenues paid by their own countrymen to help (*i*) the poorer regions of Europe, and (*ii*) the "African countries". The result is shown in the following schedule:

ANSWERS TO THE QUESTIONS "ARE YOU FOR OR AGAINST THE USE OF TAXES PAID BY:"

	Germany	Belgium	France	Italy	Luxembourg	Netherlands	Average
In order to aid the poorer regions of Europe							
For	53	49	39	45	23	76	49
Against	22	35	44	23	41	17	28
No Reply	25	16	17	32	36	7	23
In order to aid "The African countries"							
For	38	29	26	30	13	65	35
Against	35	53	56	34	54	24	40
No Reply	27	18	18	36	33	11	25

1. *Berlingske Tidende,* March 30, 1965.
2. *MacLean's,* January 23, 1965. It is not clear from this summary when the survey was made.
3. Gallup International, *L'Opinion publique et l'Europe des Six* (IFOP, Paris, 1962).

Except in Luxembourg, where there was a striking lack of enthusiasm for either of these policies, opinion seemed balanced or favourable in the case of European assistance, but there was uniformly less interest in multilateral aid to African countries. In Germany and Italy, opinion was balanced on the latter issue, in France and Belgium it was decidedly against, and only in Holland was it decidedly favourable. This is curiously at variance with the French and Belgian interest in securing the assistance of their European partners in their aid effort in their former colonies, and with the lack of enthusiasm expressed by Dutch politicians for such participation.

Conclusion

Like the very conception of "foreign aid", the idea of a public opinion about foreign aid is far from simple. Aid for whom, for what purpose, in what manner ? Citizens in Western countries are apparently not indifferent to such distinctions, and yet this is often neglected when "foreign aid" is raised as an isolated issue. It is of course true that a public opinion poll can be conducted on the basis of any question whatever, but if general and uniform questions regarding the desirability of a policy of "aid to underdeveloped countries" were put to citizens of different Western countries, the responses would undoubtedly be strongly affected by their specific image of the less developed countries, by the traditional association (or lack of it) with some part of the *tiers monde,* and by some consequent notion of a reasonable policy for which the compelling motives might be felt to lie anywhere in a spectrum ranging from the expiation of colonial and racial guilt or concerns with the international balance of power, through hopes for future economic benefits, to a genuine sense of the brotherhood of man in the face of suffering and deprivation.

IV

THE VOLUME OF AID AND ITS MEASUREMENT

The diversity of bilateral aid policy is reflected in the statistical picture of actual aid flows. First of all, the flow of financial resources to underdeveloped countries naturally varies from one industrial country to another. It will hardly do to regard this flow, whether absolutely or as a percentage of national income or GNP, as a measure of the readiness to aid, and even less of the economic burden assumed by donors, but the flow of official capital is nevertheless obviously a major aspect of aid policy. So are the directions, the terms, and the forms of assistance.

Indeed, bilateral aid does not consist in unconditional charity towards an anonymous *tiers monde,* and it might well be argued that there is more to be learned from the form it actually takes than from statements and discussions about its motives. The latter may be confused and inconclusive; but what is actually done represents the balance of the forces influencing policy.

THE FLOW OF AID

A first difficulty in the measurement of foreign aid is that aid policies consist of a whole spectrum of measures influencing economic relations with less developed countries. In regard to finance, it increases the volumes and improves the terms of capital flowing to underdeveloped countries. Such measures range from outright grants of cash, commodities, or services to guarantee schemes designed to stimulate private investments. There is no unequivocal statistical summary of such a plethora of activities, and there is no substitute for a detailed study of all the components on the flows of resources between industrial and less developed countries. This flow is exhaustively described in various OECD publications, and here it is only necessary to recall some principal features of the situation[1].

Usually, the flow of financial assistance is measured by adding up the variety of official grants and loans, excluding only very short loans on some more or less arbitrary criterion. (Purely military assistance is also excluded.) This is to focus on the short-run balance of payments aspect. From other points of view, however, grants and loans are obviously too different to add; this will be considered later.

---

1. Cf. *Development Assistance Efforts and Policies.* Reports by Willard L. Thorp, Chairman of the Development Assistance Committee (OECD, 1964, 1965); *The Flow of Financial Resources to Less Developed Countries, 1956-1963* (Paris, 1964).

In Table IV. 1, disbursements on government grants and loans are included. They are counted net of repayments, which in recent years have fluctuated around some 20 per cent of the gross value of new lending; but they are not net of interest payments (closer to 10 per cent of gross new lending) which in line with conventional balance of payments principles have been regarded as factor payments and thus belonging to the current rather than the capital balance.

TABLE IV.1. THE FLOW OF OFFICIAL FINANCIAL RESOURCES FROM INDUSTRIAL OECD COUNTRIES TO DEVELOPING COUNTRIES AND MULTILATERAL AGENCIES, 1950-1964 (DISBURSEMENTS)

Billion U.S. Dollars.

YEAR	BILATERAL GRANTS	BILATERAL NET LENDING[1]	MULTILATERAL CONTRIBUTIONS	TOTAL	YEARLY AVERAGE RATE OF GROWTH
1950-1955 (Annual Average)	1.8		0.1	1.9	
1956	2.6	0.5	0.2	3.3	
1957	3.0	0.4	0.4	3.9	15 %
1958	3.2	0.8	0.4	4.4	
1959	3.1	0.9	0.3	4.3	
1960	3.6	0.6	0.7	4.9	
1961	3.9	1.3	0.8	6.1	
1962	4.0	1.4	0.6	6.0	0
1963	4.0	1.7	0.4	6.1	
1964	3.9	1.8	0.4	6.0	

1. Maturities exceeding one year, net of amortization.

The total disbursements in the table grew rapidly until 1961 and have since then remained virtually stationary. The corresponding receipts by less-developed countries actually continued to increase, as disbursements from multilateral agencies rose while payments into them declined. New *commitments* of bilateral loans and grants also flagged in the early 1960's and were actually lower in 1963 than in 1962, but in 1964 they again increased. Lending has been increasing more rapidly than grant aid which only increased by about 50 per cent in 1956-64 while net lending more than tripled. No account has been taken in the table of the price changes for commodities purchased or supplied; this has been estimated at roughly 10 per cent since 1956, reducing the real volume of assistance correspondingly.

The terms on which loans have been made available have been eased in recent years, as illustrated by the average rates of interest and maturities in Table IV. 2, but the declining share of grant aid might be said to have worked in the opposite direction.

Occasionally, private capital movements are included in the flows of resources to developing countries, although it is explicitly recognized that it is only in special circumstances that this flow may be said to contain an element of assistance. Government guarantees or a policy of incentives may be of great importance in easing the terms and stimulating the volume of private investment to LDC's, but insofar as such policies influence private

TABLE IV.2. INTEREST RATE AND LENGTH OF MATURITY, 1961-1963.
OFFICIAL BILATERAL LOAN COMMITMENTS BY INDUSTRIAL OECD
MEMBER COUNTRIES COMBINED

Weighted Average.

YEAR	MATURITY (YEARS)	INTEREST RATE (%)
1961	18	4.7
1962	23.8	3.6
1963	24.6	3.4
1964	27.6	3.5

investment, the aid element is nonetheless official, and it is not measured by the volume of private investment or even by the volume of, say, guaranteed export credits.

In the balance of payments of industrial countries vis-à-vis less developed countries, private capital movements do, however, play a prominent role, although all indications point to a decline in the net exports of private long-term capital from industrial countries to less-developed countries in recent years. OECD estimates show them roughly constant at a level slightly higher thans $ 2.5 billion during 1956-61, and in 1962 and 1963 they declined below $ 2 billion[1]. Private export credits fall in a different category and have not usually been adequately reported in balances of payments. Guaranteed private export credits, however, have been reported to the OECD; the net amounts of such credits (for more than one year) showed no definite trend in the late 1950's, but have increased steadily since then, running at about $ 600 million in 1963.

The total of official and private long-term capital and guaranteed export credits (for more than one year) from OECD countries has thus been of the order of $8.5 billion in 1962 and 1963, and this is the "total official and private flow" reported by the OECD. The total reported by the Development Assistance Committee is slightly lower, chiefly because the DAC figures exclude lending for less than five years.

THE BALANCE OF PAYMENTS VIS-À-VIS LESS DEVELOPED COUNTRIES

It should not be thought, however, that the flow of resources just referred to has its direct counterpart in a trade balance of similar magnitude. Actually, the most striking conclusion that emerges from attempts to reconcile information about current and capital balances between OECD countries and the less developed countries is the extreme degree of ignorance that still prevails in this important domain. Table IV. 3, which is largely illustrative in purpose, points up the magnitude of the discrepancy. The "errors and omissions" items in this sketch of the situation in 1962 is almost $6 billion dollars, or as much as the total of the official flows and with the opposite sign. A large part of this is supposed to be explained by the "reverse flow" of capital from the less developed countries for which little information is available and which is not taken into account in the capital items in Table IV. 2 (or in the OECD statistics from which they are taken). Estimates of

---

1. *The Flow of Financial Resources, 1956-63*, Table IV. 4(a).

the outflow of short-term funds from developing countries, especially Latin America, based on their recorded outflow and their errors and omissions items, and guesses about unrecorded repatriation of capital by French residents in Algeria and elsewhere run as high as $2-3 billion[1]. It is, of course, also possible that the balance on current account is understated.

The second most striking thing about the balance of payment in Table IV. 3, is the smallness of the export surplus towards the developing countries. In spite of government expenditures in these countries (for administrative and military purposes) which, together with assistance expenditures and private investment and credits, provide more than 10 billion dollars, the developing countries' surplus of imports and transportation and other services from OECD member countries appears as barely $2 billion. The bulk of the gap is due to the item already discussed, but in addition develop-

TABLE IV.3. AN APPROXIMATE BALANCE OF PAYMENTS FOR OECD COUNTRIES WITH LESS DEVELOPED COUNTRIES, 1962

Billion U.S. Dollars.

Goods and Services	3.0
Merchandise trade (f.o.b.)	1.6
Investment income	3.3
Government expenditures	—2.1
Transportation, etc.	0.3
Transfers and Long-term Capital	—7.9
Official bilateral, net	—5.4
Private long-term, net	—1.9
Multilateral contributions	—0.6
Guaranteed private export credits	—0.5
Change in Liquid Assets	—0.5
Errors and Omissions	5.9

ing countries paid over $3 billion as interest and dividends to nationals in industrial countries. (Reinvested earnings are in principle included in the capital balance.)

The situation which has here been described in broad strokes is worth bearing in mind in the assessment of development assistance, but no rash conclusions should be draw from it. It first of all demonstrates the obscurity in which important aspect of international economics are still shrouded. It suggests that at present the volume of net private investment in developing countries is inferior to the flow of income from past investments out of these countries. It also suggests that the aggregate import surplus of developing countries is startlingly small even compared merely to the volume of official assistance in the forms of loans and grants. But it must not be inferred that development assistance is negated by capital flight or serves to make possible the payment of investment income to nationals in industrial countries. Very great national and regional differences are concealed behind the aggregates

---

1. Cf. the UNCTAD paper on "Financing for an Expansion of International Trade", E/CONF. 46/9, p. 69.

in Table IV. 3, and there is no apparent relationship between receipts of development assistance on the one hand and "reverse flow" or other payments on the other. There is no reason whatever to doubt that development assistance makes available considerable resources over and above those that would otherwise be at the disposal of developing countries. However, what the figures suggest is that in the absence of development assistance, the less developed countries would have a large deficit on current balance vis-à-vis the industrial countries and possibly be substantial exporters of capital rather than importers.

THE GEOGRAPHIC DISTRIBUTION OF FOREIGN ASSISTANCE

It has been stressed in the preceding sections how much historic links and especially those to former colonies have shaped foreign aid programmes. (That territories that remain in colonial status receive their assistance from their metropolis goes without saying.) Thus, in 1962, France directed 95 per cent of her official bilateral assistance to former and present colonies ; the United Kingdom 92 per cent, the Netherlands and Belgium 90 per cent. The role of strategic considerations is also evident, especially in the US foreign assistance programme, which directed 20 per cent of its bilateral disbursements in 1962 to a relatively small number of military ward countries with a total population of only 60 million (Laos, Cambodia, South Korea, South Vietnam, Taiwan, Jordan).

Together with territories that remain colonial, the new nations thus receive almost three-quarters of all grant aid and about half of official lending. Their population amounts to about 70 per cent of that of the *tiers-monde,* and in this very crude accounting their share is thus not disproportionate, but the colonial and ex-colonial nexus does involve greater emphasis on grants-in-aid. Underdeveloped countries whose independence is of old standing receive a volume of assistance largely determined by the contributions from the United States and Germany. Other contributions, while not unimportant, especially not in individual recipient countries, do not greatly affect the magnitudes[1].

The flow of official capital to underdeveloped countries is not very evenly distributed among the populations of the *tiers monde,* however. Even a broad geographic breakdown shows very great differences in the flows received per head in underdeveloped regions. In 1962, for instance, the official financial assistance per head received from OECD members was :[2]

Africa North of the Sahara	$13.6
South of the Sahara	4.4
South America	4.1
Middle East	5.0
South Asia	1.9
Far East	3.3

The question inevitably raised by such figures is to what extent a pattern of foreign aid which is heavily influenced by historical and traditional links with donor countries could conceivably be a rational and desirable allocation

---

1. See Tables IV.9-10 at the end of this chapter.
2. Extract from Table IV.13 at the end of this chapter.

of the funds available for assistance among the countries eligible to receive it. It is true that merely to pose this question is to dismiss the extent to which the essence of bilateral assistance is bilateral relationship. But in Western thought about foreign aid problems, two other principles vie for consideration along with the idea of bilateralism. One is the conception that advanced countries should contribute in an equitable manner and "share the burden" of assisting developing countries. The second is that the assistance extended to less developed countries should be distributed in accordance with their needs, taking into account the undisputed fact that the bulk of the effort must be their own. These two principles — from each donor according to his ability, and to each recipient according to his need — give rise to two sets of extremely difficult assessments. In this context, only a few of the major issues can be outlined, first those relating to burden-sharing, and secondly those bearing on "aid requirements".

BURDEN SHARING

When the overall contribution of an industrial country to development assistance is considered, whether in its international debate or international councils, it is invariably seen in relation to that of other countries. Whatever their impact, there is no doubt that the statistics on assistance to less developed countries which have been compiled and diffused by the OECD and the United Nations in recent years have entered the political debate of donor countries. The percentage of GNP represented by the flow of resources towards underdeveloped countries has become a stock-in-trade of political controversy, and especially wide currency has been given to the "target" that one per cent of GNP should be devoted to some kind of capital movement to less developed countries. This is a notion of burden-sharing which, however primitive, is a testimony to the political relevance of the conception.

There are essentially three issues : (*i*) what is the burden to be shared ; (*ii*) how is it to be measured ; and (*iii*) how is it to be allocated among those willing to shoulder it ?

In 1961, the members of the Development Assistance Group, meeting in London, adopted a resolution in which they agreed "to recommend that a study should be made of the principles on which Governments might most equitably determine their respective contributions to the common aid effort".

Among other things, it was also agreed "that the common effort should provided for expanded assistance in the form of grants or loans on favourable terms". Although the "effort" was not defined in detail, the resolution referred to development assistance alone. But, if such assistance is seen as part of a larger strategy of international diplomacy in which a common interest prevails, it might be argued that development assistance should be seen in conjunction with other categories of expenditures, such as certain military expenditures, the cost of international government, etc.[1]. If, on the other hand, it is proposed that indeed development assistance as such constitutes a joint effort in which donor countries contribute, and that the contributions ought to be equitable, "having regard to the circumstances of each country, including its economic capacity and all other relevant factors", to cite the London resolution once more, then it must be asked how the burden of development assistance should be assessed.

---

1. Cf. Edward S. Mason, *Foreign Aid and Foreign Policy*, Ch. 3.

The working definitions of the "flow of financial resources" used in OECD and UN statistics, and even in the UN resolutions, are plainly inadequate for this purpose. The sum of grants and net long-term capital movements is relevant to the analysis of the balances of payments of the parties involved, but no-one would contend that the "burden" of a loan is the same as that of a grant of the corresponding amount, or that a 7 per cent loan is equivalent to one at 2 per cent. Nor can the real cost of aid which takes the form of shipments of surplus commodities be counted at prevailing market prices. Shipments of surplus agricultural commodities by the United States amount to about 30 per cent of that country's official bilateral aid and one-fifth of total assistance from OECD members. This surplus has accumulated in consequence of a domestic policy of price support and was not originally acquired by the U.S. government in order to be distributed overseas. The sacrifice involved, therefore, depends on the alternative uses of the surpluses. If there were none but to burn them or store them indefinitely, the cost of giving them away would be nil, or even negative. When they are given away in the form of loans against local currency, the question arises, as with all loans repayable in local currency, whether holdings of such currencies will ever be used by the lender and whether they should be seen as genuine loans or a form of grants.

One way of comparing the relative burdens involved in grants and loans at different terms is to estimate the discounted present value of future amortization and interest payments. The "grant element" of a loan, computed in this fashion, will depend on the interest rate and maturity, and the grace period, if any, and on the discount rate employed[1]. The discount rate should reflect the return on public capital in optimal employment in the lending country, and it is clear that the proper rate of discount to be used in the recipient country to estimate the benefits is likely to be different, so that the real cost to the donor and real benefit to the recipient will differ[2]. It might be argued also that the discount rate should include a risk premium, and the choice of the proper discount rate cannot be made with any precision.

When the service charges on a loan are discounted by its own rate of interest, their present value equals the amount of the loan. Thus, there can be no concessionary element unless the interest rate is lower than the proper discount rate.

The longer the maturity of a loan, i.e. the longer funds are made available on concessionary terms, the greater the grant element, and a grace period postponing repayment will have the same effect[3].

---

1. For the mathematics of the problem, see the Annex. John A. Pincus used the discounting procedure in his article on "The Cost of Foreign Aid," *The Review of Economics and Statistics*, Vol. LXV, No. 4, November, 1963.

2. See Wilson E. Schmidt, "The Economics of Charity: Loans versus Grants", *The Journal of Political Economy*, Vol. LXXII, No. 4, August, 1964.

3. Tables 1-4 in the Annex show the grant element as a percentage of the face value of a loan for different maturities and grace periods, but for quick estimates an approximate formula may be used:

$$n = (q - i)(2.5 + \frac{T}{5})(1 + \frac{G}{T})$$

Here, n is the grant element, q the rate of discount, i the interest rate, T the maturity in years, and G the grace period by which amortization is deferred.

The importance of the terms of lending and of the rate at which repayments are discounted may be illustrated by a few examples. A number of economists have estimated the opportunity cost of capital in the United States at around 6 per cent[1]. Taking this as the discount rate, a loan at 5 per cent and a maturity of 10 years will have an estimated concessionary element of only 4.2 per cent of the nominal value. A development loan at 2 per cent, with a maturity of 40 years, and a grace period of 10 years, will have a grant element of 49.4 per cent. More recently, however, it has been suggested that the social rate of return to capital in industrial countries is much higher than market rates of interest, and rates between 15 and 20 per cent have been advanced for the United States and Germany[2]. If such rates were adopted for estimates of the opportunity cost of foreign aid and investment even the hardest loans would involve considerable sacrifice, and with a discount rate of 15 per cent the two loans just cited would involve grant elements of over 30 and 80 per cent respectively. However, for the purpose of reducing flows of assistance to some common basis it seems more appropriate to employ a discount rate which approximates the rate at which donor governments raise funds in their capital markets, and in the following exercises a rate of 6 per cent has been chosen. It might be noted that the discounting must be applied to gross lending rather than to the lending net of repayments included in the previously cited estimates of the flow of resources, for the essence of the practice is that loan figures are reduced by the present value of service charges associated with these very loans rather than by repayments that happen to be made on old loans. The fact that development loans are not usually disbursed all at once raises another problem. The terms of loans are reported at the time of their "commitment" but drawings may be spread out over a number of years. If the disbursement period is short relative to the maturity this problem is not major, but it must be remembered that it is commitment figures rather than disbursements that are discounted.

When the official bilateral loans of OECD member countries are thus discounted, the grant element is found to have increased rapidly in recent years as the result of the softening of terms. According to Table IV.4, the grant element almost tripled between 1961 and 1962.

The value of PL 480 shipments has been estimated by Pincus. In the officially reported figures, Title I sales (for local currency) are valued at world market prices, shipments under Titel II and III at CCC prices. Pincus attempted to determine the prices that would have prevailed in world markets if the shipments had been sold, and counted 89 per cent of the loans in local currency as grants[3]. It may be doubtful whether sale on the world market is the proper alternative to be considered, but it is at any rate logically consistent. The real cost of PL 480 shipments in 1961 is then reduced from a nominal value of $1,491 million to $651 million, or by 56 per cent.

If the total OECD assistance effort in 1961 is now revalued on these principles, the total of grants and grantlike contributions should be reduced

---

1. See, e.g. Arnold C. Harberger, "The Interest Rate in Cost-Benefit Analysis", in *Federal Expenditure Policy for Economic Growth and Stability* (Washington, 1957); Otto Eckstein and John V. Krutilla, *Multiple Purpose River Development* (Baltimore, 1959).
2. Robert Solow, *Capital Theory and the Rate of Interest* (Amsterdam, 1963). Lecture III.
3. Pincus, *op cit.*, p. 362.

from $3,950 to $3,100 to take account of the deflating of PL 480 shipments. New lending in 1961 contained a grant element of about $150 million, according to Table IV.4. Contributions to multilateral agencies may for these purposes been counted as grants and amounted to $840 million. The total estimated burden of the 1961 assistance programme of industrial OECD countries would then be about $4.1 billion. The actual flow of official grants and net lending was $6.1 billion or 0.74 per cent of combined GNP in the donor countries. The "burden" as here estimated was about 0.5 per cent of GNP.

It should be stressed that when the "burden" of assistance loans is reduced by the discounted value of future repayments, the result is not necessarily lower than the *net* lending which enters into the "flow of

TABLE IV.4. DISCOUNTED VALUE OF OFFICIAL BILATERAL GROSS LOANS FROM OECD MEMBER COUNTRIES

YEAR	GROSS LENDING	DISCOUNTED VALUE	GRANT ELEMENT
1961	$2,070 mill.	$151 mill.	7%
1962	1,890	358	19
1963	2,230	430	19

NOTE: The rate of discount was taken as 6 per cent. No account was taken of grace periods, and loans were not discounted individually. Average interest rates and maturities were applied to totals for gross lending.

financial resources". The former represents gross lending less the discounted value of future reflows. The latter represents gross lending less the current repayments on past loans. If gross lending has been increasing steadily for some time at a rate approximately equal to the discount rate, it is apparent that the discounted flow of future service charges will be about the same as the service charges on past loans. If lending is counted net of all service charges on past loans, the two measures will in fact be identical if gross lending grows at a rate corresponding to the discount rate[1]. If the current flow of lending is counted net of amortization only, it will obviously be higher. The net flow in this sense, which is the one customarily employed, will thus be superior to the estimated burden if gross lending increases sufficiently rapidly. If it does not increase steadily, or does not increase rapidly enough, the grant element in new lending programmes will be larger than the flow of net lending[2].

The terms of assistance are not the same in different aid programmes. Estimates of the real burden of individual country programmes will, therefore, not be in the same proportion to the net flows of assistance and the share of the overall burden borne by an individual country will not appear the same as when the net flows of resources are compared. The second and fourth columns of Table IV.5 show the shares in the flow of bilateral and multi-

1. Assuming linear amortization. See Annex.
2. If gross lending is assumed to grow steadily at the rate of r per cent per annum, the rate of interest is i, and the discount rate q, then the net flow will exceed the grant element if $r + i > q$. If there is to be any grant element at all, $i < q$, so it is possible that $r + i < q$, in which case the grant element will be larger. Actually, of course, development lending has not grown at a steady rate, and its terms have not remained constant.

lateral official assistance (net of repayment) in 1963 and the shares in the economic burden involved by the commitments entered into in 1963 by donor countries[1].

The first impression of a comparison between these two columns is that the procedural refinement makes fairly little difference. The share of the United States remains approximately two-thirds, those of the United Kingdom and Germany 6-7 per cent. Of the four largest donors, only France registers a significant change as the large grant content of the French aid system raises the French share from 14 to 18 per cent. Relatively speaking, however, the changes are significant for many smaller donors whose aid programmes are slanted towards grants or loans in proportions very different from the average.

Needless to say, a great many qualifications should be appended to this approach. It fastens exclusively on the real cost in terms of resources and gives no weight to balance-of-payments problems or budgetary strains. Nor does it take into consideration the possible direct benefits to donors. It pays no attention to preferential tariff or purchasing arrangements and other devices of commercial policy which may benefit less developed countries with or without a burden to the industrial one. And above all it presumes a homogeneity in the aid effort which on many counts is lacking. For donor countries the aid effort has not only a quantitative side, but direction and content as well.

But as long as the basic assumptions of burden-sharing are accepted there is nevertheless a case for assessing the economic sacrifices entered into by donor countries regardless of, say, balance-of-payments problems. Structural rigidities that limit a country's ability to shift resources rapidly into desired uses may pose serious short-run obstacles, especially when the foreign trade sector is small relative to GNP, but there is no reason to believe that a real transfer problem would prevent donors from increasing volumes of aid substantially if they were so inclined. The resource cost of an aid programme must remain one of its basic economic dimensions.

As for the principle which should guide equitable burden-sharing among donors, proportionality to GNP clearly enjoys great popularity and is by far the simplest one. However, social thought in industrial countries has long since adopted progressive taxation and a case can be made for the position that the same principle should be applied in any international assessment of contributions for development assistance. Rosenstein-Rodan has applied the U.S. income tax progression to families in industrial countries[2]. Similarly, Kravis and Davenport argue that

> for the world as a whole... the distribution of income between countries is less equal than the distribution within the developed countries and, if the choice for progressivity made by the people of the individual countries is not irrational, there appears to be a case for progressivity in international burdensharing[3].

---

1. For bilateral commitments in 1963, see DAC 1964 Review. Average terms by country are shown in *The Flow of Financial Resources*, Ch. II. Multilateral disbursements are treated as grants and added to bilateral commitments.
2. Rosenstein-Rodan, *op. cit.*
3. Irving B. Kravis and Michael W.S. Davenport, "Political Arithmetic of International Burden-Sharing", *The Journal of Political Economy*, Vol. LXXI, No. 4, August, 1963, p. 317.

TABLE IV.5. NET FLOW OF OFFICIAL RESSOURCES TO LDC's AND ESTIMATED REAL COST OF COMMITMENTS, 1963

Million U.S. Dollars.

	Net Flow of Official Resources		Estimated Real Cost of Aid Commitments	
United States	4,058	64.6 %	2,620	62.4 %
United Kingdom	413	6.6	280	6.7
Germany	421	6.7	237	5.6
France	865	13.8	739	17.5
Canada	98	1.6	52	1.2
Italy	60	1.0	14	0.3
Netherlands	38	0.6	30	0.7
Denmark	7	0.1	14	0.3
Belgium	96	1.5	92	2.2
Japan	171	2.7	94	2.2
Norway	11	0.2	21	0.5
Portugal	47	0.7	16	0.4
Total	6,285	100.0	4,209	100.0

NOTE. Bilateral official commitments from DAC, *1964 Aid Review*, p. 104. Average terms of lending for individual countries from *The Flow of Financial Resources*. PL 480 shipments were assessed in Method C proposed by Pincus. Amortization and interest payments were discounted at 6 per cent. Contributions to multilateral agencies were treated as grants in their entirety.

In experimental calculations they therefore applied progressive tax scales both to nations and to individuals. (In the latter case, the same tax rate is applied to all individuals with the same real income and the sum of estimated taxes to be levied in each particular country is taken to be that country's equitable contribution.) Real incomes were compared by means of purchasing power parities.

The result is obviously affected by the progressivity of the tax scale. According to the less progressive German rates, the assessed share of the United States (based on 1960 per capita real incomes) would be 46 per cent of the total; on the steeper United Kingdom scale it would be 70 per cent (Table IV.6). For other donors, the absolute change in percentage points is of course smaller but in relative terms the shares of some of the smaller donors are very much more sensitive to the choice of method of assessment. The most extreme case is that of Japan, where the per capita income is so low that the progressive U.K. rates would result in an assessment of only 0.5 per cent, while the German rates would give her a share of 5.6 per cent.

It is well known that purchasing power comparisons show currencies of many high income countries to be overvalued, and a proportional assessment based on money income (or GNP) will therefore contain a hidden element of progression. As Table IV.6 shows, this effect is not inconsiderable with regard to the shares of the United States and Japan.

Table IV.5, which shows the actual distribution of the flows of grants and net loans as well as of the estimated "real cost" of aid, is not entirely comparable with Table IV.6. The first refers to 1963 and includes 12 donor countries; the second is based on incomes in 1960 in ten countries (the first 12 less Belgium, Norway, and Portugal, plus Sweden). Nevertheless, the general picture is clear. The French share, however measured, was higher than any of those indicated by different methods of assessment. The United States and Japan fell between the upper and lower limits indicated by different assessments; all other countries were below. It is of course in the nature of this kind of comparison that many of them fall below their assessed shares precisely because the French share is so large.

By and large, however, it is surprising how closely the actual shares, especially of major donor countries, approximate those which different estimates of their ability to pay would indicate to be appropriate. Considering the diversity of bilateral aid, its enormous dependence on special relationships of the most varied character, the variety of motives underlying it, and the great range of types of assistance, it is difficult not to find it more remarkable that the shares in the tables match as well as they do than that great differences, particularly in relative terms, prevail for smaller donors.

TABLE IV.6. SHARES OF TEN DONOR COUNTRIES
BY VARIOUS METHODS OF ASSESSMENT

In percentage.

Countries Assessed	Proportional Taxation		Progressive Taxation of Real Incomes					
			Applied to Individuals			Applied to Nations		
	Money Income	Real Income	U.K. Rates	German Rates	U.S. Rates	U.K. Rates	German Rates	U.S. Rates
	1	2	3	4	5	6	7	8
United States	61.4	55.0	69.2	59.6	66.7	70.4	46.1	64.5
United Kingdom	8.5	9.2	7.4	8.7	7.3	7.5	11.9	8.0
Germany	7.6	8.8	6.7	8.4	6.8	7.4	11.9	7.9
France	6.5	7.5	5.6	6.7	5.6	5.8	9.6	6.4
Japan	4.7	6.8	2.4	5.4	4.6	0.5	5.6	2.3
Canada	3.9	3.6	4.0	3.9	3.9	3.8	5.2	3.7
Italy	3.7	4.8	1.8	3.6	2.1	1.2	4.3	3.5
Sweden	1.6	1.6	1.1	1.3	1.1	1.3	1.9	1.3
Netherlands	1.4	1.9	1.2	1.6	1.2	1.4	2.4	1.6
Denmark	0.7	0.8	0.6	0.8	0.7	0.7	1.1	0.8
Total	100.0	100.0	100.0	100.0	100.0	100.0	100.0	100.0

Source : Kravis and Davenport, p. 323. Calculations refer to the year 1960.

THE "REQUIREMENTS" OF FOREIGN AID

On the demand side of foreign aid, the quest for a rationale is at least as difficult. Obviously, the "need" for foreign resources in an underdeveloped country is an extremely elusive concept. It might well be argued that it is virtually unlimited whatever problems would in the short run arise from the adjustment to really massive inflows.

Generally, however, aid requirements are estimated on the assumption of some target growth rate. It is, of course, also necessary to make assumptions about the contributions that the developing country itself will be able to make, which is clearly in part an aspect of its economic policy, and about important structural parameters, which can be estimated only with a large margin of uncertainty.

Aid requirements have been estimated for individual countries as well as on a global basis. In complexity and refinement of technique these estimates range from the "jottings on the back of an envelope" to fairly detailed sectoral analyses, but in almost all cases the emphasis has been either on the need for additional capital or on the need for additional foreign exchange to meet the chosen target. The results have tended to be significantly different, as seen from Tables IV.7 and IV.8.

When external resources are seen as additions to domestic savings, the "savings gap" is estimated as the residual between capital requirements and expected domestic savings. The capital requirements have been estimated by (*i*) the capital-labour approach, and (*ii*) by the capital-output approach. In the first case, the attainment of a certain rate of growth in non-agricultural employment is taken as the target and a certain investment is assumed to be necessary to transfer a worker from the rural sector into such employment.

TABLE IV.7. SUMMARY OF ESTIMATES OF THE SAVINGS GAP

Source	Reference Data				Projection Targets				
	Reference Years	National Income (Billions of $)	Per Capita Growth in National Income Per Cent	Inflow of Capital (Billions of $)	Period of Projection	Per Capita Growth in National Income Per Cent	Capital Coefficient	Annual Foreign Capital Required (Billions of $)	Additional Foreign Capital Required (Billions of $)
	1	2	3	4	5	6	7	8	9 = 8−4
A. a) United Nations[1]	1949	97	0.75	1.0	1950-60	2.0	5.8	14.0	13.0
b) United Nations excluding China and Mongolia[1]	1949	77	...	1.0	1950-60	2.0	5.8	8.5	7.5
B. Millikan-Rostow[2]	1953	110	...	3.0	...	2.0	3	6.5	3.5
C. Tinbergen/EEC[3]	1959	128	...	4.0	...	2.0	3	7.5	3.5
D. Hoffmann[4]	1959	100	1.00	4.0	1960-69	2.0	3	7.0	3.0
E. Rosenstein-Rodan[5]	1961	192	...	4.0	1962-66	1.8	2.8	6.4	2.4
	1966	232	1.80	6.4	1967-71	2.2	2.8	6.4	—
	1971	285	2.20	5.0	1971-76	2.5	2.8	5.0	—

    1. *United Nations, Measures for the Economic Development of Underdeveloped Countries* (Sales No. 51.II.B.2). An adjustment is made in UN publication A/AC.102/5, so that mainland China and Mongolia are excluded. The estimate is made of the amount of capital needed to provide new employment outside agriculture, assuming that a fixed additional investment is required for each person added to non-agricultural employment. Further, it is assumed that the developing countries spend each year one per cent of their national income on agricultural extension services and research, and 3 per cent on other agricultural investment.
    2. Max F. Millikan and W.W. Rostow, *A Proposal, Key to an Effective Foreign Policy* (New York, 1956). The estimates of additional capital requirements are based on the absorptive capacity of the developing countries. For Latin America, the upper limit of the annual capital inflow is taken at 14 per cent, for the other developing countries at 35 per cent of gross capital formation. The assumed capital output ratio is 3.
    3. J. Tinbergen and Centre de Documentation du Comité d'Action pour les Etats-Unis d'Europe. *La Communauté Européenne et les Pays Sous-Développés* (May, 1959). The target growth rate in per capita income is put at 2 per cent (oil producers excluded); the capital output ratio is assumed to be 3.
    4. Paul G. Hoffman. *One Hundred Countries, One and One Quarter Billion People*, Washington D.C. (1960). The target growth rate in per capita income is 2 per cent; the capital output ratio is fixed at 3. As distinct from the above quoted studies, this projection combines the requirements for investment resources and the figure of foreign exchange requirements. The capital projections relate to "development capital" only.
    5. Paul W. Rosenstein-Rodan. "International Aid for Underdeveloped Countries". *The Review of Economics and Statistics*, Cambridge, Mass. (1961). The estimates are based on the absorptive capacity. The capital-coefficient applied is 2.8; capital is used in the sense of "development capital" only. The marginal savings rate is assumed to be considerably higher than the average savings rate.

In the second case, it is the capital-output ratio, i.e. the net investment required to raise output by one dollar, that provides the bridge between the target rate of growth and the required level of investment. If national income is to grow by 4 per cent a year and the capital-output ratio is 3, the required investment rate is 12 per cent of income.

Most of the estimates of the savings gap which were presented in the late 1950's indicated a shortage of $6-7 billion a year. (Table IV.7.) This, it must be noted, is about the level attained by official flows in the early 1960's.

Other estimates have focused on the gap between import requirements and export earnings. Future export earnings are usually derived from projections of the imports by developed countries of broad commodity groups for which income demand elasticities have been estimated. Import requirements in developing countries are estimated on the assumption that they are functionally related to variables like national income, output in specific sectors, volumes of investment, etc. The choice of approach must depend largely on the availability of data, but generally it is difficult to take adequate account of possibilities of import substitution, although attempts have been made to distinguish between the components of growth serving to raise domestic end use or exports and those that amount to import substitution[1].

Projections of the foreign exchange gap tend to point to considerably larger aid requirements than estimates of the savings gap. As Table IV.8 shows, the range has been between $10 and 20 billion a year, or on the average at least twice as much as the savings gaps estimated on roughly similar assumptions about desired or required growth. By definition, however, the contribution made by foreign resources to foreign exchange availability and to available savings will be identical ex post, and the discrepancy requires more comment.

It must first be admitted that very large margins of uncertainty attach to both kinds of estimates. The savings gap is extremely sensitive to the capital-output ratio and to predictions of domestic savings. The Rosenstein-Rodan estimates of capital requirements which have long represented the most detailed published estimates of this kind have been sharply criticised on these grounds. If, for instance, capital-output ratios are assumed to fall between 4 and 3 rather than between 3 and 2.5, and if marginal savings rates are assumed to be only a few per cent lower than in his calculations, the resulting requirements of foreign resources may easily be found to be twice as large[2].

Estimates of the foreign exchange gap, on the other hand, are extremely sensitive to the assumptions about import requirements and the possibilities of import substitution. The projection of future export earnings is generally considered more reliable. At any rate, different investigators tend to reach greater agreement in this respect than in others, but this is chiefly a reflection of the similarity of their methods.

---

1. See Hollis B. Chenery, "Patterns of Industrial Growth", *The American Economic Review*, September, 1960.

2. See Gisela Grimm, "Wachstumsmöglichkeiten und Kapitalbedarf der Entwicklungsländer", *Konjunkturpolitik*, No. 5-6, 1962 ; Hans-Jürgen Petersen, "Bemerkungen zu Rosenstein-Rodans Schätzungen des Kapitalschussbedarfs der Entwicklungsländer", *Konjunkturpolitik*, No. 3, 1964.

TABLE IV.8. SUMMARY OF ESTIMATES
OF THE FOREIGN EXCHANGE GAP

Source	Year of Reference	Year of Projection	Import Requirements	Export Earnings	Trade Gap	Service Gap	Foreign Exchange Gap
			Billions of Dollars				
GATT[1]	1956-1960	1975	28-32	17	11.15	...	...
UN[2]	1959	1970	41.0	29.0	12.0	8.0	20.0
G. Blau/FAO[3]	1959	1970	41.0	31.0	10.0	8.0	18.0
B. Balassa/OECD[4]	1960	1970	38.0	33.0	5.0	5.5	10.5
	1960	1975	48.7	41.9	6.8	6.9	13.7

1. *International Trade, 1961.* General Agreement on Tariffs and Trade, Geneva, 1962. The trade-gap has been calculated at 1956-1960 prices. In the figure quoted, the predicted export of manufactured goods is not taken into account. According to an estimate of Balassa this counterbalances the assumed price difference. The GATT study assumes a 5 per cent growth in GNP for Latin-America and Asia and 1.5 per cent for Africa.
2. *United Nations, World Economic Survey, 1962.* Part I, New York, 1963. The UN study assumes a growth of 5 per cent of GNP. The figures are expressed in 1959 prices. Current trends and policies are assumed unchanged.
3. Gerda Blau, *Commodity Export Earnings and Economic Growth.* Royal Institute of International Affairs, London (1963). The figures quoted are one of three alternatives (varying from 14 to 20 billion), assuming possible effects of favourable changes in trends and policies for all items other than primary export earning. Average unit value of imports by 1970 has been assumed to be increased by 10 per cent, relative to average unit value of exports, which is held constant. The average growth rate is fixed at 5 per cent.
4. B. Balassa, *The Problem of Growth in Less Developed Countries and its Significance for OECD Policy.* Special Report III: Trade Prospects for Developing Countries, OECD, 1963. The figures given reflect the alternative where target rates of income growth were realized in the world economy.

It has occasionally been suggested that the two approaches should be used as cross-checks, or that since both purport to measure essentially the same thing, the one least liable to estimation error should be used[1]. But the issue is not merely statistical. The two gaps correspond to the projected internal and external disequilibria that would be generated by growth. One is essentially determined by capital requirements and the marginal savings ratio; the other by import requirements and export possibilities. There is no reason why, ex ante, these two gaps should be equal. Ex post on the other hand they will be identical, and the two hypothetical processes on which the two projections are based cannot both come true. If, for instance, the foreign exchange gap is larger than the savings gap, and foreign assistance capital is made available in sufficient amounts to meet the latter, import requirements cannot be met as expected (assuming that export earnings and other regular sources of foreign exchange have been correctly predicted). External balance will be attained by a number of adjustments, one of which is likely to be a fall in the rate of growth. If, on the other hand, assistance covers the larger foreign exchange gap, an excess of savings will tend to arise which might lead to increased consumption, a fall in domestic savings and a low marginal savings ratio. (This, incidentally, may cause the impression of inadequate self-help performance.) It must be stressed that the process of adjustment by which the ex ante gaps are reconciled can take a great variety of forms, and

1. See Bela Balassa, "The Capital Needs of the Developing Countries", *Kyklos,* Vol. XVII, No. 2, 1964.

that this aspect of the transfer problem in developing economies has so far been inadequately studied.

In this context, it is only necessary to stress that the role of foreign resources may, to simplify matters, be said to be that of breaking one or the other of the bottlenecks to growth that are met in inadequate supplies of capital and foreign exchange[1]. Several years ago, Reddaway suggested that in the case of India, "the need for aid on balance payments grounds is greater than the need of saving grounds"[2], and recent estimates by aid agencies suggest that this is the case in most underdeveloped economies. This is also in line with the tendency already cited for estimates of the foreign exchange gap to be larger than those of the savings gap. In other words, the capacity for domestic capital formation appears in many countries to be more adequate for growth than their ability to increase export earnings.

How does the actual distribution of capital flows to developing countries compare with the requirements estimated by the methods referred to above ? The answer cannot be simple. On the one hand, there are self-evident and spectacular discrepancies, notably in the case of military wards which in addition to strictly military support tend to receive very large amounts of economic assistance. On the other hand, if these cases are neglected, there is a rather pronounced similarity between the patterns of actual official capital flows and the requirements as estimated by Rosenstein-Rodan a few years ago. The rank correlation between the two for the countries included in Table IV.14 is as high as 0.79. Most of this effect, however, is due to the fact that large countries receive more aid. When the patterns of per capita assistance received and required are compared, there is practically no correlation at all. But, as in the case of the supply of aid, which appears more closely related to ability to pay than the complexities of bilateral aid would make one expect, the distribution of assistance among underdeveloped countries also appears somewhat less unrelated to needs than the procedures and policies for the giving of aid would seem to guarantee. Among the forces that presumably serve to bring this about are the requests and the sollicitations for assistance by receiving countries. For an understanding of how the international aid system operates, the distribution of assistance and the factors that affect it should obviously be studied.

---

1. For more extensive discussions of this problem, see, e.g., Hollis B. Chenery and Michael Bruno, "Development Alternatives in an Open Economy", *The Economic Journal*, Vol. LXXII, No. 285, March, 1962 ; Hollis B. Chenery, "Foreign Assistance and Economic Development", paper presented to the Econometric Society in Boston, 1963 (roneo.) ; P.I. McKinnon, "Foreign Exchange Constraints in Economic Development and Efficient Aid Allocation", *The Economic Journal*, June, 1964.

2. W.B. Reddaway, *The Development of the Indian Economy* (London, 1962), Appendix D., p. 216.

TABLE IV.9. GEOGRAPHIC DISTRIBUTION OF OFFICIAL BILATERAL GRANTS FROM OECD MEMBER COUNTRIES TO DEVELOPING COUNTRIES, 1962

U.S. Million Dollars.

Donor Countries	To Former/Present Colonies: Of Donor	To Former/Present Colonies: Of Other Donors	To Independent Countries	Unallocated	Total
France	750	—	—	22	772
United Kingdom	184	7	15	9	215
Belgium	63	—	2	1	66
Portugal	3	—	—	—	3
Netherlands	41	—	—	1	42
Italy	12	1	21	1	35
United States	29	585	568	157	1,339
Germany	—	13	76	19	108
Japan	—	68	4	3	75
Canada	—	27	..	—	27
Norway	—	1	..	—	1
Denmark	—	—	1	—	1
Sweden	—	2	1	—	3
Switzerland	—	—	—	2	2
Austria	—	—	..	—	—
Total	1,082	704	688	214	2,688
Percentage of grants	40	26	26	8	100
Percentage of population	70		30	—	100
Per capita ($ U.S.)	1.75		1.60	—	1.84

Table IV.10. GEOGRAPHIC DISTRIBUTION OF OFFICIAL BILATERAL NET LENDING FROM OECD MEMBER COUNTRIES TO DEVELOPING COUNTRIES, 1962

U.S. Million Dollars.

Donor Countries	To Former/Present Colonies: Of Donor	To Former/Present Colonies: Of Other Donors	To Independent Countries	Unallocated	Total
France	85	—	10	13	108
United Kingdom	154	1	11	—	166
Belgium	—	—	3	—	3
Portugal	38	—	—	—	38
Netherlands	5	—	—1	—	4
Italy	—	—4	47	—	43
United States	27	216	437	—	680
Germany	—	84	113	41	238
Japan	—	33	53	—	86
Canada	—	—	20	—5	15
Norway	—	—	—	—·	..
Denmark	—	—	—	—	..
Sweden	—	—	—	—	—
Switzerland	—	—	—	—	—
Austria	—	—	5	—	5
Total	309	330	698	49	1,386
Percentage lending	22	24	50	4	100
Percentage population	70		30	—	100
Per capita ($ U.S.)	0.62		1.62	—	0.95

Table IV.11. PER CAPITA OFFICIAL BILATERAL GRANTS FROM OECD MEMBER COUNTRIES, 1962

U.S. Dollars.

Recipient Countries	France	Belgium	United States	Italy	Netherlands	United Kingdom	Portugal	Germany	Japan	Canada	Sweden	Norway	Denmark	Total
Present or Past Colonies:														
French	7.54	—	2.77	—	—	0.05	—	0.02	0.15	—	—	—	—	10.53
Belgian	—	3.12	0.35	—	—	—	—	—	—	—	—	—	—	3.47
U.S.	—	—	0.88	—	—	—	—	—	0.30	0.03	—	—	—	1.21
Italian	—	—	0.74	0.52	—	0.13	—	0.04	—	—	0.04	—	—	1.47
Netherlands	—	—	0.14	—	0.42	—	—	—	0.22	0.01	—	—	—	0.79
U.K.	—	—	0.37	—	--	0.25	—	0.01	0.03	0.03	..	..	—	0.69
Portuguese	—	—	—	—	—	—	0.23	—	—	—	—	—	—	0.23
Independent countries:	—	..	1.32	0.05	—	0.04	—	0.18	0.01	—	..	—	..	1.60

TABLE IV.12. PER CAPITA OFFICIAL BILATERAL LENDING FROM OECD MEMBER COUNTRIES, 1962

U.S. Dollars.

Recipient Countries	Portugal	France	United States	United Kingdom	Belgium	Netherlands	Italy	Germany	Japan	Canada	Austria	Total
Present or Past Colonies:												
Portuguese	2.85	—	—	—	—	—	—	—	—	—	—	2.85
French	—	0.86	0.17	0.01	—	—	—	0.05	—	—	—	1.09
U.S.	—	—	0.82	—	—	—	—	—	0.03	—	—	0.85
U.K.	—	—	0.26	0.21	—	—	-0.01	0.10	0.04	—	—	0.60
Belgian	—	—	—	—	0.15	—	—	—	—	—	—	0.15
Dutch	—	—	0.10	—	—	0.05	0.01	—	0.03	—	—	0.19
Italian	—	—	0.04	—	—	—	—	—	—	—	—	0.04
Independent Countries:	—	0.02	1.01	0.03	0.01	..	0.11	0.26	0.12	0.05	0.01	1.62

TABLE IV.13. PER CAPITA ASSISTANCE TO DEVELOPING COUNTRIES PER REGION FROM OECD MEMBER COUNTRIES, 1962

U.S. Dollars.

Recipient Region	Capital Assistance Per Capita				
	Grants	Net Loans	Loans Repayable in Recip. Curr.	Transfer of Resources	Total
Europe	1.9	1.3	1.1	0.9	5.2
Africa	4.4	1.2	0.1	0.7	6.4
a) North of Sahara	8.9	1.5	0.4	2.8	13.6
b) South of Sahara	3.1	1.1	0.1	0.1	4.4
America	1.2	2.2	0.2	0.3	3.9
a) North and Central	1.0	0.8	0.3	..	2.1
b) South	0.7	2.8	0.1	0.5	4.1
Asia	1.2	0.5	0.3	0.6	2.6
a) Middle East	3.2	1.0	0.2	0.6	5.0
b) South	0.4	0.6	0.4	0.5	1.9
c) Far East	2.1	0.2	0.2	0.8	3.3
Total	1.8	1.0	0.3	0.6	3.7

TABLE IV.14. NET OFFICIAL CAPITAL FLOW FROM OECD COUNTRIES AND MULTILATERAL AGENCIES COMBINED IN 1962[1] AND CAPITAL AID REQUIREMENTS ACCORDING TO ROSENSTEIN-RODAN[2]

U.S. Million Dollars.

Recipient Country	Inflow		Requirements		Inflow		Requirements	
	Total	Rank	Total	Rank	Per Capita	Rank	Per Capita	Rank
Turkey	217	21	172	20	7.59	17	5.93	22
Yugoslavia	174	18	129	17	9.16	20	6.79	23
Greece	35	2	45	12	4.38	9	5.63	20
Libya	33	1	2	1	33.00	23	2.00	8
Egypt (U.A.R.)	194	20	143	19	7.19	15	5.30	19
Morocco	91	14	20	8	7.58	16	1.67	7
Congo (Leopoldville)	82	13	5	3	5.47	13	0.33	1
Tunisia	55	9	10	4	13.75	21	2.50	9
Tanganyika	49	5	10	5	4.90	12	1.00	4
Kenya	50	6	5	2	5.56	14	0.56	2
Port. Overseas Prov.	39	4	12	6	3.25	7	1.00	5
Bolivia	36	3	18	7	9.00	19	4.50	16
Brazil	189	19	283	21	2.52	5	3.77	14
Chile	135	17	33	10	16.88	22	4.13	15
Argentina	97	15	104	16	4.62	10	5.00	18
Colombia	73	12	71	14	4.87	11	4.73	17
Venezuela	71	11	45	11	8.88	18	5.63	21
Mexico	54	7	100	15	1.46	2	2.70	10
Iran	63	10	67	13	3.00	6	3.19	12
India	742	23	1,578	23	1.64	3	3.48	13
Pakistan	391	22	292	22	4.03	8	3.01	11
Indonesia	114	16	142	18	1.16	1	1.45	6
Thailand	54	8	24	9	1.93	4	0.86	3

$$r = 1 - \frac{6\Sigma\,(D^2)}{N\,(N^2 - 1)}$$
(rank)

0.79   0.28

1. Source: OECD statistics.
2. Rosenstein-Rodan, *op. cit.*

V

FORMS OF FINANCIAL AID

Of all the forms of development aid, technical assistance seems to have the most immediate appeal to donor countries. Small aid programmes show a marked preference for such contributions — the despatching of experts and teachers, the training of foreign students, peace corps projects, etc. — and they are sometimes said to be more "efficient" than financial assistance. If this were really thought to be so, then aid funds should of course be shifted towards more technical assistance. Actually, however, the greater share of the flow of assistance to underdeveloped countries takes the form of financial assistance to finance investment projects or programmes. The share of bilateral asssistance officially categorised as "technical co-operation" is about 15 per cent, and the share of multilateral assistance devoted to this purpose is somewhat larger. It is true that all capital projects involve considerable elements of "the transfer of skills", in project preparation and execution, the training of operating personnel, etc., and that this constitutes an intangible but no less valuable aspect of many private investment projects. Consequently, the share of official assistance devoted to the transfer of skills and knowledge rather than conventional goods and services might be assessed at approximately one-fifth.

The problems and strategy of technical assistance are of immense complexity. Although the critical issues are sometimes sociological or psychological, sometimes technologic, important questions about the economic returns to different and alternative activities also arise. So far, however, relatively little is known about the economic returns to knowledge and skills in underdeveloped countries, and even such basic issues as the relative priorities of elementary and higher education in development strategy remain controversial.

Technical assistance will therefore be left to specialised discussion, but some of the principal questions concerning the forms of financial assistance will be considered in this chapter as they tend to be raised in most discussions about foreign aid. To a large extent such discussions about loans versus grants or about tied and untied aid have focussed on the value of different kinds of aid to receiving countries. But different forms of aid also impose different burdens on donors. A tied loan, or a grant out of a surplus disposal programme, mean a smaller sacrifice than a straight grant of the same amount in convertible currency.

Rational aid policy must mean a search for forms of aid that achieve their effect at a minimum cost, or maximise their effect at given level of sacrifice. Such calculations may not be possible, but there is nevertheless reason to ask which principles are reflected in the forms of development assistance as currently practiced.

Loans and Grants

Although the bulk of the development assistance by OECD countries consists of grants and grantlike contributions, the role of lending has increased rapidly. In 1956, about 20 per cent of the bilateral gross flow of assistance consisted of lending: in 1963, this share was over 35 per cent and almost 50 per cent of new commitments took this form. But the role of lending in the aid systems varies widely among donor countries. In France, and in smaller countries, whose aid consists mostly of technical assistance, it is fairly minor; in Italy, Japan, and Germany, on the other hand, it accounts for more than two-thirds of the total flow.

Loans are made on widely differing terms, and there is actually a whole scale of assistance of different hardness — from straight grants, and soft 40 or 50-year loans at token interest rates, to export credits for 5 years carrying interest rates of 7 per cent or more. Grace periods and waivers of various kinds add to the gamut.

It is doubtful whether this variety of terms reflects any valid rationale. A number of different principles are usually evoked when then terms are set or explained, but none are compelling. In the first place, it is often held that the terms should be related to the purpose or the project for which the aid is intended. Grants are thus by some donors reserved for technical assistance, soft terms are taken to be appropriate for improvements like roads and harbours and other infrastructure projects which do not yield any direct revenue, and hard terms for projects of greater pecuniary profitability. There are many objections to this principle : it is simply not appropriate to base economic planning on the assumption that each project should pay for itself, or that it should get the type of finance for which it can pay. Whatever the risks attaching to individual projects, they do not apply to government loans. The capital costs charged by the borrowing government against its own projects, or from private borrowers, if the funds are re-lent, need have no relationship with the rates charged by the lender, and this is occasionally recognised, as in the two-step lending procedure increasingly used by the United States and some other governments.

It is striking to what extent the practices of lenders and donors vary on this point. The United States has a rich spectrum of hard and soft types of aid, but ordinary, repayable loans tend to fall into either a soft category of development loans (AID loans), or a hard one (mostly Export-Import Bank). French development finance has been largely in the form of grants, whatever the uses, but the financial assistance outside the franc area is in the form of credits. The EEC Development Fund started its operations supplying only grants but has recently shifted into lending. German assistance, on the other hand, tends to take the form of loans of a wide range of interest rates and maturities. UK loans have had a rate of interest based on the government's borrowing rate plus a management charge; loans have been made softer by lengthening maturities and grace periods and by waivers of interest payments which left nominal rates intact while reducing the effective cost of borrowing; in June, 1965, it was announced that this practice would occasionally be extended to a waiver of all interest payments.

Secondly, terms are influenced by the relationship between the assisting and the receiving country. Grants are much more common to colonies and ex-colonies than to other countries. In 1962, for instance, bilateral assistance to former and/or present colonies of the donor contained only 22 per cent net loans; other bilateral aid 42 per cent. In part, this reflects the fact that, in the context of "special relationships", aid tends to be of a different character altogether: general programme aid and budgetary support is given almost exclusively to ex-dependencies and in grant form. But, clearly, it is also a widespread view that capital assistance in the form of grants expresses a generosity and a confidence appropriate only where the links to the recipient are especially intimate.

According to a third set of arguments, loans are generally superior to grants as a form of foreign assistance as the obligation to repay is assumed to discourage waste and impose a salutary economic discipline on recipients. The implication is that governments of developing countries use funds irrationally, and that repayment obligations will achieve a more rational use of funds than the pressure of scarcity alone. But if governments are assumed to be irrational, then even though they may service their loans there is no presumption that they will use them particularly rationally[1].

It is also asserted that loans are politically preferable in that they make the aid relationship reciprocal and businesslike and thuis spare the sensibilities of recipients, while gifts humiliate and offend. Such arguments were especially common when soft Soviet loans were described as politically more effective than United States aid, which in the middle of the 1950's still contained only grants and relatively hard loans.

From a strictly economic and fairly abstract point of view, the issue may be seen as a matter of the relative productivity of capital. If capital can be more productively employed in the recipient economy than in the country supplying the aid, the transfer results in an overall gain for both economies combined, and this gain is larger the greater the volume of the aid. The benefit to the recipient will consist of this gain plus the concession the donor may make by providing the funds at a lower rate of interest than the yield available to him in domestic uses of funds. This concession is the only burden to the donor: it is proportional both to the volume and to the margin of "softness" so that the burden will remain constant if the volume of lending is increased while interest rates are raised appropriately. It can then be shown rigorously that the objective of maximising benefits with a given burden will be achieved by "hard" — but also very large — loans. If on the other hand capital is less productively employed in the recipient economy than by the donor, the two countries combined will suffer a loss by the transfer. The benefit to the recipient will then fall below the burden to the donor by the amount of this loss, which again will be proportional to the volume of the transfer. As the smallest volume compatible with a given burden arises from a straight grant, the conclusion is that in this case the benefits associated with a given "sacrifice" will be maximised by grant aid. According to this argument, aid should thus be supplied either in the form of hard loans or grants, depending upon the relative productivity of capital in the two eco-

---

1. Cf. Wilson E. Schmidt, "The Economics of Charity: Loans versus Grants", *Journal of Political Economy,* Vol. LXXII (August, 1964), p. 386.

nomies involved, and there is no room on rational grounds for intermediate terms[1].

Tho these considerations, the force of events has added an overriding one: the ability to service external debt. The terms of aid should on this view be determined, or at least tempered, by the debt servicing capacity of the individual recipient. The indebtedness of underdeveloped countries is said to be so large that softer terms of development assistance are necessary. Lenders supplying credit on soft terms find it offensive if others supply it on harder terms, thus "pre-empting" debt servicing ability, and the question of terms thus becomes one of joint interest to the donors.

"Debt servicing capacity" is in this context an ambiguous concept. It might well be argued that a country that qualifies for foreign assistance has no debt servicing capacity at all. Debt service competes with essential imports for foreign exchange earnings which are regarded as insufficient, and with investment needs for inadequate savings. When debt is serviced in such a situation, it is in recognition of the fact that fulfilment of obligations is a prerequisite for further assistance, but no-one excepts a country in this position to liquidate its external debt.

As long as assistance continues, donors as a group may thus be said to pay their own service charges. If a constant or growing resource gap in the underdeveloped countries is to be met by the net flow of development loans, the growing reflow will require gross lending to increase at a faster rate the harder the terms, and the ratio between gross lending and net inflow will soon become very large. The magnitudes involved may be illustrated by a simple example. If the net flow of resources to underdeveloped countries is to grow at 5 per cent per annum and this is to be met by loans at 5 per cent or 2 per cent, the gross lending and the debt burden will increase according to the following schedules[2]:

Interest Rate		5 per cent		2 per cent	
Year	Net Flow	Gross Lending	Indebtedness	Gross Lending	Indebtedness
			In Billion Dollars		
0	1.00	1.00	0	1.00	0
5	1.28	2.24	6.4	1.77	4.1
10	1.65	3.80	16.5	2.85	10.0
15	2.12	6.90	31.8	4.32	18.3
20	2.72	10.90	54.4	6.32	30.0
25	3.49	16.60	87.5	8.97	45.6
30	4.49	24.70	134.9	12.61	67.6

1. This brief summary takes no account of the complications arising from repayment terms. When these are considered the conclusion paradoxical at first, is that even when hard loans are indicated they are best given with very long maturity, in the limit as perputual loans. In other words, repayment terms should be soft although interest should be hard. The explanation, in terms of the above argument, is that *if* the postulated differential between the marginal yields to capital persists, the consequences of the transfer are only accentuated by an extension of the time during which it applies.

2. See the model in the Annex. The debt burdens are independent of the maturities; the gross lending required is affected by them in the early years, and for these calculations it was assumed that both loans were amortized at 10 per cent on outstanding debt each year, corresponding roughly to a 20-year maturity.

If assistance loans are given only for distinct projects, repayment may well put a strain on the balance of payments and raise a demand for balance of payments support and consolidation credits to "roll over" the debt. Actual debt service crises arise from unforeseen short-term developments: a bunching of repayment obligations, a sudden drop in export earnings, a failure to restrain imports, etc. A high debt service ratio will increase the risks of such crises if creditors are not willing to continue lending, but, as experience has shown, countries can manage their balance of payments with very high long-term debt service ratios, and it would be impossible to specify a permissible maximum for debt service. The tolerable limits depend on policies of lenders as much as on those of the borrowers[1].

For donor countries as a whole, then, the question of the terms of aid is in the long run a choice between a large gross flow of loans with a substantial reflow, and a smaller flow of grants or softer aid, with the same net effect on the balance of payments. Although it may be said that, in fact, donors themselves pay the service charges on loans, the point is precisely that they usually do not do so directly. The gross flow of assistance, over which they tend to have some control, may be tied to specific types of projects and exports. The reflow of service charges will certainly reduce the import capacity of the borrowing country, but it will not necessarily reduce imports from the donor in question.

To individual countries therefore the problem does not appear in the same light as to donors as a whole. As long as it is accepted that underdeveloped countries will not become net capital exporters until much progress has been made towards more rapid growth and higher levels of living, there will be no repayment and reduction of overall external debt. But individual lenders may expect repayment and reconsider their aid policies, or shift their lending to other countries. Especially to the extent that development lending is used for export promotion, but also when it serves other purposes of the donor, loans may thus to have great advantages over a policy that would devote to assistance only the smaller amounts corresponding to the "real burden", but in grant form.

External indebtedness of many underdeveloped countries has indeed grown rapidly in the course of the last decade. Thus, the "public debt" of India has risen from $310 million to $2,936 million between the end of 1955 and 1962, and that of Pakistan from $147 million to $829 million. An IBRD study of these problems estimates that the service on public debt for 74 countries, including most of the underdeveloped world, amounted to $2.9 billion in 1963, of which $2.2 billion in amortisation and 0.7 in interest. With a wider definition of external debt, including commercial arrears and similar, the author concludes that debt service obligations of these countries are no less than $4 billion and could have well reached $5 billion per annum[2].

There is, of course, nothing surprising about the fact that indebtedness of the underdeveloped countries has risen rapidly. With net lending at several billions a year, the world system of assistance is bound rapidly to produce a debt of colossal magnitude. This may in itself discourage further lending and

---

1. Cf. Dragoslav Avramovic *et al.*, *Economic Growth and External Debt* (Baltimore, 1964).
2. *Ibid.*

slow down the volume of assistance. It also raises fundamental problems about the nature of assistance in the form of lending.

Banking is not commonly regarded as a charitable activity, no matter how useful its services. A repaid loan on commercial terms is not considered a loss, and such benefits as the borrower derives from it he also pays for. Development banking, like all forms of banking, serves to reduce risks by improving the organisation of the capital market and thus improve the terms on which credit is available. When it is nevertheless financed by voluntary subscriptions in capital markets, it cannot very well be described as an activity involving a sacrifice. Its contribution is the improvement of terms, and it is not measured by the gross volume of lending.

Characteristically, official development loans of all kinds are extended "when no other sources of finance are available", and in a great number of instances they are extended on terms covering the cost of raising the capital — with the use of the superior credit worthiness of governments or respected banking institutions, such as the World Bank. If the ultimate lenders supply their funds voluntarily, the burden must be nil. The use of official credit to help developing countries is cheap in such circumstances.

If the borrowing country has access to no alternative lender, or if the terms are better than those offered elsewhere, the benefit may indeed be very great. In the case of hard loans at World Bank rates, this assumption is no longer accurate. There may now be said to exist at least an imperfect market for development loans, which, especially when they serve export promotion purposes, are not hard to raise for sensible projects and within the framework of the international aid system it is not correct to assume that developing countries lack alternative sources of finance.

Concessionary loans are indeed another matter, but even these are not gifts, and the "burden" of such loans on the donor economy must, as argued in the previous chapter, be assessed in terms of the magnitude of the concession.

From a banking point of view, there is no reason why productive and remunerative projects should not be financed by loans, provided that the flexibility of the receiving country in managing its resources is sufficiently great to enable it to transfer the service charges, or this necessity is alleviated by the steady growth of further loans. But in the perspective of development policy, lending inevitably raises serious problems. However they are estimated, the "requirements" of developing countries are considerable and will remain so for a long time. It is unlikely that very many countries will be able to, or even allowed to, turn themselves into net capital exporters for a very long time. Some models of the development process assume that capital imports into underdeveloped countries on concessionary terms will stop within a reasonably short time if self-sustained growth has been achieved, and that accumulated development debts could then be repaid. However, by that time, the gap between rich countries and poor will be even more overwhelming than it is to-day, and it seems more than doubtful that the factors underlying foreign aid will have lost their urgency. It is sometimes assumed that finance on conventional terms and from private sources will become increasingly easy. But developing nations, saddled with enormous debts and fixed charges, will, by traditional standards, be miserable credit risks. Indeed, it is hard to believe that, even if continued official aid dwindles to a halt, the next phase would not be a moratorium on debts falling due.

A few years ago, Ragnar Nurkse, speaking about international grants-in-aid, said: "Interest payments, from poor to rich, are now, it seems, not only basically unwanted by the rich countries, but indeed are felt to be somehow contrary to the spirit of the age". Events have not proved him right. So far, it is principally in the help of rich countries that grants have been given precedence. Not only in war finance and lend-lease, but also and most spectacularly in the Marshall Plan, recourse was had to grants in order to avoid the later complications of the transfer of repayments to a nation which was wrongly suspected of being intrinsically a creditor country. For similar wisdom to prevail in the field of development finance, the readiness to shoulder a real burden must be considerably greater in donor countries than it is to-day.

The role of foreign investment in the past is sometimes cited as a precedent to current development assistance, but such a comparison suffers from a number of weaknesses. To begin with, although there is general agreement that the intangible contribution of foreign investment to the transfer of technology was of great importance, the quantitative role of foreign investment in capital formation seems to have been surprisingly small, except during very short bursts[1]. Even these sufficed to raise the share of debt servicing in the balances of payments of the borrowers to very considerable proportions, and almost every burst of investment produced its painful aftermath of crisis.

Above all, however, it should be stressed that the classical cases of overseas investment before World War I did not involve a sustained transfer of resources to the debtor countries but precisely the opposite. The reflow of investment income to creditor countries almost from the start matched or exceeded the flow of new net investment. This was notably true in Britain where, in Imlah's words, "foreign investments... were a little like a revolving fund, a large part of the income was re-invested in the further development of other lands[2]". Before 1870, the balance of interest and dividends reflects the balance on current account fairly closely, and in the remaining decades before 1913, investment income was vastly greater than capital exports. Interest on foreign investments then represented about 10 per cent of British national income; 4 per cent of national income was invested overseas in 1870-1913 — a staggering ratio by some measures, but only 40 per cent of the income from past foreign investment[3]. The evidence on French foreign investment is conjectural but such as it is it points to a rate of growth from the beginning of the 19th century distinctly below the probable rate of return[4].

Needless to say, this picture conceals complex geographic shifts in the gross flow of capital and, from the point of view of the borrowers, the situation was sometimes different, as it had to be. Thus, during the sharp burst of foreign investment in Canada during the period 1900-1913, net imports of capital rose rapidly from rough equality with payments of investment income, and over the period as a whole, investment income paid was only slightly more than one-third of total capital imports.

---

1. Cf. Kenneth Berrill, "Foreign Capital and Take-off", in W.W. Rostow (ed.) *The Economics of Take-off into Sustained Growth* (1963).
2. Albert H. Imlah, *Economic Elements in the Pax Britannica* (Cambridge, Mass., 1958), p. 60.
3. A.K. Cairncross, *Home and Foreign Investment, 1870-1913* (Cambridge, 1953) Ch. I.
4. Rondo E. Cameron, *France and the Economic Development of Europe, 1800-1914*, (Princeton, 1961), p. 79.

Generally speaking, however, it remains true that in the heyday of foreign investment, flows of capital only rarely and intermittently grew at a rate sufficient to offset the flow of interest and dividends in the opposite direction.

Much 19th and early 20th century investment was directed to territories capable of developing their export sectors and foreign exchange earnings, so as to be able to meet repayment obligations without difficulty, and crises were due to speculative excess. But in those countries which failed to develop their exports, chronic strains tended to arise in the balance of payments.

Historically the contribution of foreign investment to the propagation of growth, significant though it was, was not that of creating a large and sustained net inflow of foreign exchange. That, however, is what development assistance efforts in the financial field aim to achieve. Provided that lending increases sufficiently rapidly, it is, of course, theoretically feasible, but the implications are serious. If lending is to create a genuine increase in available resources, the debt must grow faster than the rate of interest on old debt. If this rate of interest is higher than the rate of growth of national income, debt must thus grow faster than national income, and service charges are likely to grow faster than export earnings and to absorb an increasing share of them.

In the traditional view of foreign investment, there is no reason in principle why foreign investment could not be serviced as long as the investment is profitable enough and as long as there is sufficient flexibility in the economy to generate the export surplus for repayment. But when the point of departure of the discussion is the premise that foreign resources on a large scale will be necessary over a long period of time to close the gap between the capital and/or foreign exchange required for growth and the domestic resources available, a number of caveats are in place. Unless loans are made on very long terms, they will have to be frequently converted or succeeded by renewed borrowing. As service charges come to claim a larger share of foreign exchange, it becomes difficult to meet them out of free, i.e. earned, exchange and a pressure to borrow to pay interest and to support the balance of payment arises. Consolidation credits and general balance of payments support already figure in many aid programmes and may be expected to become more frequent in the future, but this development will lend new content to the issue of project vs. programme aid.

PROGRAMMES AND PROJECTS

Whether aid should be made available for specific projects or in a way that leaves the recipient free to dispose of it more freely is a question which has been frequently discussed ever since the problems of development assistance began to receive specific attention. When donor countries first exchanged their views on this subject, colonial and ex-colonial powers stressed the value of general budgetary support while many other donors insisted that project aid was necessary to assure the efficient use of aid funds. In the United States, a preference for project aid has recently yielded to an increased stress on programme aid for allocation within the framework of a general plan satisfying the donor both in regard to its conception and its implementation.

It has often been remarked that such control over the use of aid is futile as an attempt to control the allocation of resources in the lending country, as long as a large sector of the economy is outside the control of the lender. It is true that, where administrative effeciency is low, project control may offer the only assurance that the loan is not used wastefully. On the other hand, it may distort the development effort if assistance is only to be had for projects of a high foreign exchange content. Vital areas of, say, agricultural development, which entail mostly local expenditure, may be neglected if assistance cannot be counted on for these purposes. On the other hand, imported equipment may be used wastefully where local resources could and should be employed[1].

To a large extent, this discussion hinges on problems of administration and planning. These will not be reviewed here. It is, however, important to realise that, apart from grants for technical assistance or general budgetary support (in ex-colonies), the bulk of development assistance takes the form of loans earmarked for specific projects, as this underlines the uncertain position of the conception of foreign aid between traditional modes of international finance and a deliberate transfer of resources to meet a "gap" in less developed countries.

When the project evaluation by a lender represents a constructive help to planners in less developed countries, as has notably been the case in the IBRD's pioneering work in project preparation, it is clearly a contribution to the borrower as well as a guarantee that funds are not ill-used. But the problems of evaluating isolated projects in overall plans, especially if they relate to infrastructure, are well known, and it would probably be desirable that lenders were readier to supply assistance on general criteria of performance. This is so for at least three reasons :

i) The preparation of special project applications for prospective donors puts a heavy strain an scarce planning resources, and in conjunction with their evaluation it is time-consuming and holds up the use of appropriated aid funds ;

ii) Even when, as at present, there may be a dearth of projects suitable for assistance, the need for foreign exchange for the implementation of a development programme may be very real ;

iii) No traditional conception of basing foreign investment on the revenue profitability of a specific project is pertinent to government-to-government loans, as the ability to repay is a function of export performance and general availability of aid and finance rather than of individual project success.

Aid-Tying

While the resort to project aid is largely meant to influence the use of resources in recipient countries, the "tying" of aid is caused by concern with the donor country's economy. The two restraints do not necessarily go together, but about two-thirds of all bilateral aid to underdeveloped countries is actually "tied" in the sense that it either consists of aid in kind in the form

---

1. For an early comment on the project approach see the IMF mission report to the government of India in 1953, *Economic Development with Stability*.

of commodities — principally U.S. agricultural surpluses — or that it is to be spent in the donor country.

The objective of such practices may be to promote exports and employment, or to protect a weak balance of payments, but their actual effect is hard to assess. It is clear that often aid would have been spent in the donor country anyway, either by virtue of traditionally close commercial relations, or because it is extended for a project for which the donor country is specially equipped to furnish materials. When not superfluous, the tying may be ineffectual, as when the receiver uses tied funds for imports that would in any case have been made, thus freeing foreign exchange for other purposes.

Finally, it must be recalled that there is little point in comparing tied aid with untied aid if it is unlikely that the aid would have been provided at all, or in the same extent unless it were tied to exports. This may well be the case if the donor country is troubled by its balance of payments, or suffers from unemployment and surplus capacity, or if the linking of aid to the donor's products seems innocuous and natural to public opinion or vital enough to exporters to become a political condition of support for an aid programme.

That untied aid would, in principle, be preferable from the receivers' point of view is quite clear. The restriction of competition involved in tying may mean that equipment is bought at higher prices, or lower quality, especially when the aid is also linked to a specific project. This need not mean more than that the real value of the aid is overstated. What is more serious is that the tying of aid aggravates the evils of limiting it to the foreign-exchange components of projects. When tied aid looms large in foreign exchange availability, there will be a tendency to distort development programmes in favour of projects with a high and special import content, while vital projects involving mostly local expenditure are neglected. Or, if they are undertaken, they might give rise to an indirect import demand that cannot be met.

When tying is a deliberate means of promoting specific exports, developing certain markets, of employing surplus capacity, donor countries can hardly be expected to renounce its use entirely. Tied aid is better than no aid, and the assistance effort cannot suffer from taking into account the mutual convenience of the partners.

Yet, many governments declare, as the British in the White Paper of 1963, that "although we tie part of our aid, we are prepared to take part in any genuine international move towards the untying of aid[1]. To proceed alone to untie aid is said to be impossible as long as other donors continue to tie theirs in ways that promote their exports and markets. There are good political reasons for such hesitation, and this is, as the Chairman of DAC has emphasised, an appropriate area for collective action by donor countries. But when, as is often the case, the reason given for tying is balance-of-payments difficulty — as in the tightening of the procurement regulations for AID loans since 1959 — the situation is not so clear.

If it is assumed that underdeveloped countries accumulate no foreign exchange reserves, then industrial countries should not in the aggregate suffer any balance-of-payments deterioration as the result of their financial assistance. Aid should take the form of a transfer of goods and services and there

---

1. *Aid to Developing Countries*, p. 13.

would be no drop in gold or foreign exchange reserves[1]. The impact of the aid policy of any one donor country on her own balance of payments will chiefly depend on what happens to that fraction of the aid which is **not** spent with the donor, but in another industrialised country[2]. These exports from third countries will induce further trade in ways determined by their import content and their effects on incomes and prices. What cannot be assumed is that, in the end, such third countries will necessarily spend their increased holdings of the original donor's currency. They may increase their reserve position, and, however that is done, it will be at the expense of the reserves of the original donor country.

There would be no reason to expect the trade flows induced by aid to leave balances of payments neutral, and the present international monetary system is admittedly deficient in mechanisms for speedy correction of balance of payments disequilibria. It is understandable, therefore, that it should be suggested that countries in balance-of-payments difficulties may legitimately tie their aid while other countries have no such excuse[3].

American procurement restrictions actually only rule out the spending of assistance funds in other industrialised countries, and so at least do not hamper trade among underdeveloped countries. A system for tying funds actually appropriated for local expenditures has also been devised by the United States. But whether or not the tying of aid actually achieves the object of relieving the balance of payments will depend both on responding by third countries and on the repercussions on commercial trade. If the main result were a corresponding displacement of commercial exports, there would be no change either in trade patterns or in the balance of payments of the donor. Actually, the possibilities of substitution are never perfect, and usually the displacement of commercial exports is probably offset by the increase in responding that results from tying, but the net effects are clearly smaller than often imagined. When aid is dispensed in areas with traditionally very close links to the donor, as French aid in the franc zone, most of it will be spent in the donor country without formal tying procedures, and it is in the nature of project assistance that the same will often be the case when projects are prepared in close collaboration with technicians from donor countries. It also stands to reason that the gains from tying are likely to be the greatest where the donor's traditional share of the market has been small, and these are precisely the cases in which most countries tie their aid if they only tie part of it — thus the ex-colonial powers generally do not tie their aid to their ex-dependencies but do in lending to countries they have not formerly assisted. Aid from the Soviet bloc is tied but, in addition, the service charges on bloc loans may be said to be tied the other way by the commitment to accept local currency or stipulated export commodities in repayment. If balance of payments problems in donor countries justify the tying of aid, it might well be argued that the far more disturbing balance of payments prob-

---

1. Even if it is assumed that aid leads to an expansion of output with a certain import content, or, if there is no spare capacity to inflation in donor countries that spills over into imports from the underdeveloped bloc, this will be offset by the spending of such export earnings.

2. The switching of resources into aid exports may, of course, raise imports of raw materials, but in this case it is not to be taken for granted that these will give rise to "responding" and be completely offset by exports.

3. Walter S. Salant et al., *The U.S. Balance of Payments in 1958*, p. 188.

lems of recipients would justify such bilateral measures to facilitate repayment[1].

Proposals have also been made to "take development aid out of the balance of payments" by trying to ensure that third countries would eventually respend aid funds rather than add them to reserves[2]. No doubt such arrangements would remove one of the obstacles to increasing aid appropriations in donor countries. But the inconveniences attaching to aid tying are very hard to estimate and are clearly exaggerated when reference is made only to the proportion of aid funds subject to procurement restrictions, for the effect of these restrictions is far more marginal than it indicates. When it is further considered that tying often provides the vital impulse for assistance and may serve other purposes besides balance-of-payment protection, it may well be asked whether the practice deserves the opprobrium it often receives. Here, as in all facets of assistance policy, it must be rational to attempt to minimise donor's inconvenience at given level of benefit. When objections to aid tying come from competing industrial countries which fear the disturbance of normal trade and feel excluded from the market created by aid funds, intricate issues may indeed arise, but the commercial interest of one country cannot constitute a valid objection to the generosity of another.

Summary

Capital assistance to underdeveloped countries takes different forms and it is not always clear what the rationale, if any, behind the spectrum of assistance might be. In fact, the terms and types of aid seem in large measure determined by a melange of administrative doctrines and rules of thumb, ad hoc political pressures, traditional banking principles, and the influence of practice in other donor countries.

Only three basic issues were raised in this chapter. (*i*) The criteria usually given for the choice between loans and grants were found to be fairly arbitrary. Thinking about capital aid is clouded by the conflict between the tradition of international finance on banking criteria and the assumptions of development assistance. International lending to underdeveloped countries had already in many cases created staggering debt burdens and if a sizeable foreign-exchange gap in underdeveloped countries is to be met over some period of time, recourse to lending, even on fairly soft terms, is bound to create serious difficulties. (*ii*) The increasing burden of service charges in the balance of payments will intensify the demand for assistance that is not tied to the foreign exchange component of specific investment projects. Project assistance offers opportunities for national identification and some check on efficiency in the small, but development plans will be less rather than more effective if they are distorted in favour of projects with high foreign-exchange content and against local-cost expenditures of great priority. (*iii*) Similar risks arise from the tying of aid to procurement in the donor country, but against the inconveniences caused to recipients must be set such genuine gains as might accrue to donors. Although the strenghthening of the balance of payments that is

---

1. V.N. Bandera, "Tied Loans and International Payments Problems", *Oxford Economic Papers*, Vol. XVII, July, 1965, pp. 299-308.
2. E.g. the suggestions by Professor Kiyoshi Kojima. See *The Economist,* July 25, 1964, pp. 401-402.

achieved by aid tying is often smaller than commonly assumed, some relief may be expected in this respect, and other motives for tying aid are among the very motives for maintaining bilateral aid programmes at all. Procurement restrictions undoubtedly make possible a larger volume of assistance than would otherwise be forthcoming and they cannot very well be regarded as intrinsically evil.

VI

TOWARDS A CODE OF DEVELOPMENT ASSISTANCE ?

This report has been at pains to stress the diversity of policies of foreign aid and the wide range of underlying circumstances and motives[1]. Generalisations about the development assistance of industrialised countries to less developed ones easily breed the impression that there is a uniform policy towards the *tiers-monde* at large in which advanced countries contribute varying amounts, such as in the case of multilateral assistance programmes operated by international organisations. Criticism of bilateral aid programmes sometimes simply amounts to the reproach that they do not sufficiently partake of the character of multilateral aid. But the variety of objectives and practices that mark actual programmes of development aid is probably neither a weakness nor a fault: it is in the first place the inescapable consequence of the fact that decisions about public uses of resources fall upon national governments, and secondly it is a factor of strength without which the flow of funds to the poorer countries would be a good deal smaller than it is.

It would also be misleading to overlook the elements of uniformity in the international aid system and the forces that serve to strengthen them. There are first of all the basic historical aspects of the situation. Whatever the reasons which in individual countries seem most compelling for the launching of a policy of development assistance, this fundamentally novel type of economic diplomacy is a consequence of the pervasive change in the relationship between industrial countries and the *tiers-monde* that the end of the colonial era has wrought. To those deeply concerned with the political stability of the world, the ultimate purpose of economic co-operation with the less developed countries must be to prevent anarchy and inflammatory crises. This concern may not be the direct determinant of aid policies in all advanced countries. Yet, foreign aid policies are to some extent forced upon aid-giving countries by the very existence of the new states.

As these policies are novel and the reasons for them in individual cases complex, so the administration of them reflects the uncertainty about where they belong — in foreign policy or in economic policy, with diplomats, Treasury officials or ex-colonial servants ? Although the outcome of the administrative response to the new tasks is not everywhere the same, the

---

[1]. Cf. E.S. Kirschen, "Objectifs et détermination de l'aide aux pays sous-développés", *Cahiers économiques de Bruxelles*, No. 24, 1964, pp. 451-471.

trend is nonetheless towards specialisation and specialised agencies. This too makes for increasing uniformity. The fact that the objectives of aid, whatever its motives, directly aim to contribute to the development of the recipient countries inevitably makes foreign aid a highly technical task and raises the demand for new categories of professional government servants.

International example and co-operation, especially in the Development Assistance Committee, has already exerted a considerable influence on technical aspects of development assistance. A code of behaviour for development assistance has implicitly taken shape, and donor governments are perfectly aware of it even when their policies are at variance from it.

What the experience of a decade of development assistance has brought home most sharply is perhaps the limits to the power of foreign aid and the overhelming importance of political and economic efforts in the less developed countries themselves. One should not expect the political and social prerequisites for rapid growth to be brought about easily — in that case, there would be little call for an international aid policy. But development assistance can at best be only a complement to self-help. The response to the recognition of this fact has so far been an increasing attention to ways in which the distribution of aid could be made to serve as a system of incentives. It is also becoming clear that a need of great priority is for assistance in the use of assistance.

But if development assistance is to meet the hopes put upon it, it is desirable that recipients and donors alike arrive at a clearer conception of the aid relationship. The mutual involvement to which development assistance gives rise is alien to the relations between sovereign states, and the difficulties of coming to terms with it are no less on the receiving side than on the donor side, probably even a good deal greater. That the aid relationship is delicate need not be repeated, but upon this fragile link rests the effectiveness of aid. If development assistance is to remain a prominent international institution for many decades to come, it will require a code of behaviour not only for donors but for all those involved, a code which needs for its emergence not only a basis in joint interests but a clear understanding of the functions and potential contributions of foreign resources. This, in the end, is the chief justification for focussing the attention of research on this major aspect of the economic relations with the *tiers monde*.

Annex

THE GRANT ELEMENT IN DEVELOPMENT LENDING, AND THE GROWTH OF SERVICE CHARGES

When loans are made on concessionary terms, these may be said to comprise an aid element, and it is reasonable to wish to estimate this grant element in cash terms and regard it as the sacrifice (or benefit) associated with such loans. The natural definition of the grant element is the difference between the face value of a loan and the present value of all future repayments (amortisation and interest payments), discounted at a proper rate of interest[1].

Interestingly enough, the expression for the grant element turns out to be very similar to another measure that arises in problems of international capital flow, namely the net outflow of resources when a flow of steadily growing gross lending is offset by the reverse flow of service charges. It is easy to see why this should be so: in the first case, current lending is reduced by the discounted value of future repayments on current loans, and in the second case it is reduced by the present value of repayments on past loans, with the rate of growth playing the same part as the discount rate in the first case.

This formal symmetry between the two problems makes it convenient to discuss them together, especially as the necessary tables will serve both types of calculations. The problem will first be posed with reference to the task of finding the net discounted value of a concessionary loan.

THE GRANT ELEMENT

The choice of the proper discount rate cannot, in the absence of an integrated world capital market, be the same if the attention is focussed on the sacrifices of the lenders and on the benefits of the borrowers. In the first case, a rate expressing the prevailing long-term yield on public capital is an appropriate measure of the opportunity cost of public loanable funds. In the second case, the alternative rates available to borrowers in underdeveloped countries are more elusive: their access to free capital markets is sporadic. In any case, the long term rate that would represent the borrowers' opportunity cost is clearly a good deal higher than that which pertains to the lenders.

---

1. Cf. John A. Pincus, "The Cost of Foreign Aid", *Review of Economics and Statistics*, XLV (1963), pp. 360-367.

The present note is only concerned with the formal aspects of the problem: given the terms of a development loan and an appropriate rate of discount, how can the concessionary element readily be estimated[1]?

Public loans of the kind we are here concerned with typically provide for a grace period of a certain number of years during which no repayment of principal is made. Thereafter, principal is usually repayable in equal instalments, although other amortisation principles are occasionally followed. In the case of certain United Kingdom loans with maturities of 25 years and grace periods of seven years, interest payments are also waived during this grace period, which obviously reduces the effective rate of interest.

In the following, it is for convenience assumed that amortisation and interest payments are made continuously, rather than at discreet intervals of six months or a year. We use the notation:

L	face value of the loan
P	present value of future repayments at time of lending
$p = P/L$	present value as share of face value
$S = L-P$	subsidy or grant element
$s = S/L$	grant element as share of face value
i	rate of interest
q	rate of discount
T	maturity
G	grace period
D	net indebtedness

In the first place, it may now be observed that, if the rate of interest is not concessionary, there can be no grant element in the sense in which the term is used here. The grace period and the amortisation schedule, no matter how important they may be in other respects, will not alter the fact that the discounted present value of repayments will equal the face value.

The outstanding debt at time t is $D(t)$, interest payments, therefore, $i\,D(t)\,dt$, and amortisation payments — $\dot{D}(t)dt$. The present value of these payments, discounted at a rate q, is:

$$P = \int_0^T (i\,D(t) - \dot{D}(t))\,e^{-qt}\,dt \tag{1}$$

As $D(0) = 0$, partial integration gives:

$$P = L - (q-i) \int_0^T D(t)\,e^{-qt}\,dt \tag{2}$$

With a rate of discount different from the interest rate of the loan, a grant element will arise, and it will depend on the mode of amortisation. I assume that during the grace period, G, there is no repayment of principal but that principal is then repaid in equal instalments in the remaining years of the loan, at a rate of $\dfrac{1}{T-G}$. During the first G years, only interest payments

---

1. In Wilson E. Schmidt's paper, "The Economics of Charity: Loans versus Grants", *Journal of Political Economy,* August, 1964, which appeared after the completion of this note, the discrete formulas for present cost are derived, though without consideration of grace periods.

are made; their present value is:

$$P_1 = \int_0^G i L\, e^{-qt}\, dt = \frac{i}{q} L (1 - e^{-qG}) \qquad (3)$$

The present value of the repayments of principal and payments of interest made after the grace period is:

$$P_2 = \int_G^T \left[\frac{L}{T-G} + i L \left(1 - \frac{t-G}{T-G}\right) \right] e^{-qt}\, dt \qquad (4)$$

which is easily shown to be:

$$P_2 = \frac{i}{q} L\, e^{-qG} + \left(1 - \frac{i}{q}\right) L \frac{e^{-qG} - e^{-qT}}{q(T-G)} \qquad (5)$$

Adding P_1 and P_2 gives the solution for this case. If the present value is written as a proportion of the face value:

$$p = \frac{i}{q} + \left(1 - \frac{i}{q}\right) \frac{e^{-qG} - e^{-qT}}{q(T-G)} \qquad (6)$$

If there is no grace period, i.e. $G = 0$, this reduces to:

$$p_0 = \frac{i}{q} + \left(1 - \frac{i}{q}\right) \frac{1 - e^{-qT}}{qT} \qquad (7)$$

or:

$$s_0 = \left(1 - \frac{i}{q}\right) \left(1 - \frac{1 - e^{-qT}}{qT}\right) \qquad (8)$$

For very short-term loans, qT is fairly small, and as an illustrative approximation one may expand e^{-qT} in series and drop the terms beyond the second power. This reduces (8) so that the grant element is simply:

$$s_0 = 1/2\, (q - i)\, T \qquad (9)$$

In other words, the concession in regard to the rate of interest is applied to the average balance of the loan over the term of maturity.

Generally, however, this approximation is not permissible, and the formula used to estimate the grant element in long-term loans with a grace period is (6), or more correctly, its complement:

$$s = \left(1 - \frac{i}{q}\right) \left(1 - \frac{e^{-qG} - e^{-qT}}{q(T-G)}\right) \qquad (10)$$

In Tables 1—4, this expression has been calculated for loans of 10, 20, 30 and 40 years maturity, with grace periods of 0, 5 and 10 years.

The tables actually show great regularity, and when the discount rate is not too high, it is possible to use the following rules of thumb:

Each concession of one percentage point in the interest rate (below the discount rate, seen as an alternative for the lender) gives rise to a grant element of:

4 per cent of the face value for a 10-year loan;
7 per cent for a 20-year loan;
9 per cent for a 30-year loan, and
10 per cent for a 40-year loan.

A grace period wil increase the grant element by the proportion G/T. Take as an example a loan given at 3 per cent, rather than a prevailing normal rate of 6 per cent, maturing in 20 years and with a grace period of 5 years. The grant element will be:

$$3 \times 7 \times (1 + \frac{5}{20}) = 26\%$$

which is in accordance with Table 2, which shows 25.5 per cent.

An even more approximate way is to use the following formula:

$$s = (q - i)(2.5 + \frac{T}{5})(1 + \frac{G}{T}) \qquad (11)$$

The simplicity of this formula is gained at some sacrifice of precision, but it is serviceable in the relevant range[1]. To illustrate, a 10-year loan at 4 per cent, discounted at a rate of 6 per cent, will contain a grant element of

$$(6 - 4)(2.5 + 2) = 9 \text{ per cent.}$$

The correct figure is 8.3 per cent, according to Table 1. A 30-year loan with a 5-year grace period, carrying an interest rate of 3 per cent and discounted at 6 per cent has a discounted present value of

$$(6 - 3)(2.5 + 6)(1 + 1/6) = 30 \text{ per cent.}$$

The correct ratio, according to Table 3, is 30.5 per cent. A soft development loan of 40 years maturity, a 10 year grace period, and a 2 per cent rate of interest, discounted as in the other cases at 6 per cent, gives:

$$(6 - 2)(2.5 + 8)(1 + 1/4) = 52 \text{ per cent}$$

while the actual figure in Table 4 is 49.4.

If not only amortisation but interest as well is waived during the grace period, a direct and substantial grant element will, of course, arise, whatever the rate of discount. Its present value wil be that of P_1 in (3). Thus, for a loan of the type given by the United Kingdom, a maturity of 25 years, a grace period of 7 years and a rate of interest of 5.5 per cent, this waiver amounts to a grant element of 31.2 per cent, even if 5.5 is taken as a normal market rate so that no concession is involved on that account — which is, more or less, the principle on which the interest on United Kingdom loans has been set.

Such a waiver may, of course, alternatively be seen as a reduction of the effective rate of interest. The effective rate of interest may be said to be that rate of discount which would make the present value of the remaining flow of repayments equal to the face value. That present value is expressed by P_2 in (4), and the effective rate of interest will be that q which makes

---

[1]. When the grace period is relatively short compared to the maturity, expansion of (10) shows that it can be written as:

$$s = (q - i)(1 + \frac{G}{T}) \frac{1}{q} (1 - \frac{1 - e^{-qT}}{qT})$$

Now, $\frac{1}{q}(1 - \frac{1 - e^{-qT}}{qT}) = T(\frac{1}{2} - \frac{1}{3!}qT + \frac{1}{4!}q^2T^2 - \ldots)$

but when $qT > 1$, this series converges very slowly. However, when $q = 6$ per cent, a least-squares fit over the range between 10 and 40 years gives the linear approximation $2.45 + 0.205\ T$.

$P_2 = L$. For the loan described in the previous paragraph, the waiver of interest payments during the grace period turns out to reduce the effective rate of interest from 5.5 to 2.75 per cent.

THE GROWTH OF SERVICE CHARGES

When borrowing is resorted to in order to cover a persistent gap in the balance of payments, the reverse flow of service charges will make it necessary to increase the amounts borrowed if the net inflow is to be maintained or grow.

Domar's classical study of the relationship between the inflow and outflow was occasioned by concern with the opposite problem: was it possible to maintain a flow of American capital exports resulting in an export surplus, or would it soon be swamped by what Professor Viner called "the wondrous working of compound interest" and returning payments of interest and amortization[1]? Domar's conclusion was that, if the flow of capital exports was growing at a constant rate, the ratio between the inflow and the outflow would eventually be stabilized at a ratio which depended on this rate of growth and the interest rate. If the rate of growth of the outward flow was greater than the interest rate, the net outflow would remain positive, but otherwise there would in the end be a net inflow.

The Domar analysis is, of course, applicable to the plight of borrowing countries whose mounting service charges are currently receiving much attention. The terms of government lending to underdeveloped countries are being softened in order to relieve the strains on their balances of payments. Such strains are often made particularly acute by the bunching of repayment obligations or by disturbances elsewhere in the balance of payments. To study the consequences of a steadily growing inflow of borrowed capital on homogeneous terms is, therefore, to simplify considerably. It nevertheless serves the purpose of illuminating the role not only of the interest rate, but also of the other terms of lending that figure in the current debate, notably the repayment period and the grace period.

The notation is as in the previous section, with the following additions:

$L = L_0 e^{rt}$ Gross flow of loans
r Rate of growth of new loans
A Amortization
I Interest payments
N Net flow $(L - A - I)$
$n = N/L$ Net/gross ratio

If we assume that the flow of borrowed funds begins at time zero and that indebtedness is at that time zero interest payments will be made until the grace period of the first loans has elapsed. Therefore, for $t < G$

$$I = i \int_0^t L(t-x) \, dx = i \int_0^t L(t) \, e^{-rx} \, dx$$

so that

$$I = L \frac{i}{r} (1 - e^{-rt}) \qquad (12)$$

---

1. Evsey D. Domar, "The Effect of Foreign Investment on the Balance of Payments", *American Economic Review*, XL (Dec. 1950), pp. 805-26.

At time G, amortisation will begin on the early loans [at the rate of $1/(T-G)$] and interest charges on those loans will fall with the outstanding debt. For $G < t < T$, we have:

$$A = \int_G^t \frac{L(t-x)}{T-G} dx = L \frac{e^{-rG} - e^{-rt}}{r(T-G)} \tag{13}$$

Interest payments on recent loans whose grace period has not lapsed will be as before:

$$I_1 = i \int_0^G L(t-x) dx = L \frac{i}{r} (1 - e^{-rG}) \tag{14}$$

but for earlier ones, we now get:

$$I_2 = i \int_G^t L(t-x) \left(1 - \frac{x-G}{T-G}\right) dx \tag{15}$$

Combining these, we have for this interval:

$$I = L \frac{i}{r} (1 - \frac{e^{-rG} - e^{-rt}}{r(T-G)} - \frac{T-t}{T-G} e^{-rt}) \tag{16}$$

Finally, when time T is reached, the first loans will have been completely amortised. The ratios of the service charges to current lending will from this time on remain constant, and they are found by substanding T for t in the expressions above.

Subtracting the service charges from the gross flow, we get the following ratios for the net/gross flow ratio for the three periods:

$t < G \qquad n = 1 - \frac{i}{r}(1 - e^{-rt})$ \hfill (17)

$G < t < T \qquad n = (1 - \frac{i}{r})(1 - \frac{e^{-rG} - e^{-rt}}{r(T-G)}) + \frac{i}{r} \frac{T-t}{T-G} e^{-rt}$ \hfill (18)

$t > T \qquad n = (1 - \frac{i}{r})(1 - \frac{e^{-rG} - e^{-rT}}{r(T-G)})$ \hfill (19)

The last expression is identical with that derived in the previous section for the grant element — formula (10) — with the substitution of the rate of growth of new loans, r, for the rate of discount, q. It shows that the net flow will eventually become negative if the rate of growth of new loans is lower than the rate of interest, and that this will be true regardless of whether maturities and grace periods are lengthened, although such measures obviously will have the effect of slowing down the return flow. The limit values for n which are reached at time T can be studied in Tables 1—4.

Actually, the approximate formula (11) derived for the grant element may be used to derive the net/gross ratio at time T. At time zero, the ratio is unity, and between 0 and T declines in almost linear fashion. Using the same numerical examples as earlier, a flow of 10-year loans increasing at a rate of 6 per cent per annum and carrying an interest rate of 4 per cent, will after ten years lead to a stable net flow of 8 per cent of current lending, while 92 per cent will be returning in the form of service charges. Already about five years after the beginning of this lending, about half of it should be offset by interest and amortisation. A flow of thirty-year loans with a 5-year grace period and 3 per cent interest, growing at 6 per cent, leads to a stable ratio around 30 per cent, but this is reached only in 30 years. The "half-time", when half of it is eaten up by service charges, is about five-sevenths of 30, or some 20 years. Lending at such soft terms as 40 years maturity, 10 year grace periods and 2 per cent interest would, if the loans grow at 6 per cent, yield a ratio of almost exactly 50 per cent, and the flow of service charges would thus never exceed half the gross of new loans.

For short term credits, of 5 years duration or less, the approximate formula (9) is more appropriate. With the substitution of r for q, we have:

$$n = (r - i) \frac{T}{2} \qquad (20)$$

Thus, a flow of 5-year export credits expanding at a rate of 7 per cent per annum and carrying an interest rate of 6 per cent produces a net inflow of 2.5 per cent, but, if loans are growing at a rate of only 5 per cent a year, there will instead be a stable outflow of the same proportion.

Short-term credits are attracting much attention in the discussion of the debt burden of underdeveloped countries. One could sometimes get the impression that export credits merely because they are of high rates and short maturities aggravate the balance of payments situation of the borrower. But, assuming that imports financed in this way are essential enough to be carried out anyway, this is only true if they grow at a slower rate than the rate of interest. If they grow faster, they actually support the balance of payments by a small fraction. If the exports in question are paid for in cash, their payment arrangements bring no relief to other claims on the balance of payments, whereas a flow of export credits will either relieve the situation or strain it further. In either case, the effect is small, and the alarm about short-term credits is often misplaced when the alternative would be a payment on such short delay that it would not on any definition be considered to belong in the capital balance, but rather in the current accounts. The conception that they seriously pre-empt servicing capacity on the public loans granted for development purposes is not self-evidently correct. If they grow fast, it should not necessarily be cause for alarm, for this is precisely when they will on the whole support the balance of payments.

We have so far followed the practice of assuming that borrowing (or lending) followed a steady path with a constant rate of growth. The net flow in that case declines steadily until a stable ratio, positive or negative, is reached. But suppose that the purpose of borrowing is to close a gap which is constant or growing. Obviously, the gross flow must then expand at an increasing rate, although ultimately it might reach a growth path where the net flow is stable and adequate to meet the requirements assumed for it. This will only be possible if the net flow actually remains positive.

This case illustrates the cascade effect that may arise in borrowing for stabilisation or development. Suppose that a balance-of-payments gap of B is growing at a steady rate, k, and is to be covered by net proceeds of borrowing, so that:

$$N = B_0 e^{kt} = L - A - I$$

What will be the necessary growth path for L? The answer is easily seen if we remember that $L - A$ is the increment per unit of time of the outstanding debt, D, to which the rate of interest is applied. The previous equation thus reduces to:

$$B_0 e^{kt} = \dot{D} - iD$$

The solution of this differential equation is (if $D(0) = 0$):

$$D = B_0 \frac{e^{kt} - e^{it}}{k - i}$$

If $k \neq i$, the larger of the two will eventually dominate the growth of the debt which will then accumulate at that rate — either at the rate of growth of the "requirements gap" or, if the rate of interest is higher, at that rate. If $k = i$, this expression is not determinate but the usual ways of finding the limit for D when k approaches i, we get:

$$D = B_0 t \, e^{kt}$$

In other words, the ratio between the debt and the *current* gap is directly proportional tot he time elapsed since borrowing began: after two years, it is twice as large, after ten years, ten times as large, etc.

How L grows depends on the amortisation method. With straight-line amortisation, as in the previous section, the problem is difficult to solve analytically. But, as Domar showed, it seems to make little difference which amortisation method is actually followed. The simplest procedure is to compute amortisation as a constant fraction, a, of the outstanding debt. Although this is rarely or never done in practice, it gives a good idea of the nature of the problem. The unpaid balance of each individual loan will then decline as e^{-at}. It will never really reach zero, but for an approximate way of relating a to the maturity, or repayment period of loans we may arbitrarily regard a loan as repaid when a balance of 10 or 20 per cent remains. The exponents of e^{-at} corresponding to these values (the logarithms) are 1.6 and 2.3, and we might for simplicity suggest:

$$a = \frac{2}{T}$$

It should be remembered that this method of amortization makes the repayment burden of a loan particularly heavy in its early years, which is precisely the opposite of grace period practices.

With these qualifications, we can write:

$$L = \dot{D} + aD$$

$$L = B_0 \frac{(a+k)e^{kt} - (a+i)e^{it}}{k - i}$$

As in the case of D, eventually the larger of k and i will dominate, so that lending will be dominated by the current needs of the borrower only if these grow faster than the rate of interest. If these needs are constant or slow to change, it is the rate of interest itself that will more and more determine the rate at which gross lending will grow. In the first case, the ratio between net and gross lending will approach a stable level, as in the previous section:

$$k > i \qquad n = \frac{k - i}{k + a}$$

This corresponds exactly to Domar's expression for the limit ratio[1]. But, if the interest rate is the larger of the two magnitudes, service charges will inevitably come to absorb more and more of the capital inflow. The ratio between net and gross flows will decline incessantly, as shown by:

---

1. Domar's R is the ratio of the backflow to the outflow, rather than the ratio of net to gross outflow, so that $R = 1 - n$.

$$N/L = \frac{i-k}{(a+i)\,e^{(i-k)t} - (a+k)}$$

which eventually approaches zero. As recalled from the previous section, there will be a net inflow only as long as new loans grow at a rate higher than the rate of interest, and it is only because new loans will reach very large volumes that the falling fraction of net resources will be adequate to cover the gap which is, it should be recalled, also increasing.

If $k = i$, then new loans will grow as
$$L = B_0 e^{kt}(1 + (a+k)t)$$
and
$$n = \frac{1}{1 + (a+k)t}$$
which will steadily diminish.

The rate of growth of new lending will in the general case be:

$$\frac{\dot{L}}{L} = \frac{k(a+k)e^{kt} - i(a+i)e^{it}}{(a+k)e^{kt} - (a+i)e^{it}}$$

as t grows, the rate of growth will, as we have already seen, asymptotically approach k or i, whichever is the larger, and it is easily shown that when they are identical, L will eventually grow at that rate.

The most relevant conclusion is that — as is intuitively seen — at the beginning, gross lending will have to grow at much higher rates if it is to cover both the need for net resources and mounting service charges. At $t = 0$, the rate of growth will be:

$$\frac{\dot{L}}{L_0} = a + i + k$$

i.e. the sum of all the three rates that occur in the calculations. In other words:

If a growing resource gap is to be met out by borrowing, new loans must be taken up at a rate that at first is the sum of the rate of growth of the needed resources, the rate of interest, and the rate of amortisation.

If there is a "planning gap" which increases at 5 per cent per annum, if average rates of interest are 5 per cent, and if average amortisation comes to another 5 per cent, borrowing would at first increase by as much as 15 per cent a year. An increasing fraction of new lending would be absorbed by service charges and the need for new lending will grow steadily larger in relation to the gap it is meant to cover.

This will be the case, a fortiori, if interest rates are higher than the growth rate of the gap. Only if interest rates are lower will service charges eventually come to constitute a stable fraction of new lending.

Interestingly enough, none of these conclusions are affected by the rate of amortisation. No matter how long the repayment periods, service charges will eventually behave as described, although it will take longer and gross lending will not have to grow quite so fast. Even this latter effect seems rather slight. In the simple case when k and i are both 5 per cent, the rate of growth of new lending ($\dot{L}/L$) at the outset is strongly affected by changes in a, but after a few decades the rate of amortisation makes very little difference:

"Maturity"	a	TIME			
		10	20	30	40 Years
10 years	0.2	30 %	12 %	9 %	8 %
20	0.1	20	11	9	8
40	0.05	15	10	8	7
∞	0	10	8	7.5	7

Even if repayments are deferred indefinitely, lending will grow at much the same rate fairly soon.

It is unlikely, in view of this, that grace periods, whatever momentary relief they provide, genuinely affect the long-term aspects of mounting indebtedness that this simple mathematical model is meant to illuminate.

So far, we have focussed on gross lending in order to be able to combine the service charges the way it is usually done whenever there is concern about debt servicing capacity. But the statistics on development lending, as in OECD documents, generally only give net lending — net, that is, of repayments, though not of interest payments.

The previous analysis becomes even simpler if we choose net lending in this sense as our main variable, for this eliminates altogether the need to discuss amortisation. We derived a simple expression for D, the total debt outstanding, and the net lending required — call it K — will simply be the rate of change in D:

$$K = L - A = \dot{D} = B_0 \frac{ke^{kt} - ie^{it}}{k - i}$$

and, when $k = i$:

$$K = B_0 (1 + kt)e^{kt}$$

The rate of growth of net lending required will be:

$$k \neq i \qquad \frac{\dot{K}}{K} = \frac{k^2 e^{kt} - i^2 e^{it}}{k e^{kt} - i e^{it}}$$

$$k = i \qquad \frac{\dot{K}}{K} = \frac{k(2 + kt)}{1 + kt}$$

At time zero, the rate of growth will be $k + i$ in analogy with the conclusion in the last section. This may seem more self-evident than the fact that the rate of required growth will be steadily declining, asymptotically approaching the larger of k and i.

Table 1. GRANT ELEMENT IN LOANS OF 10 YEARS MATURITY

Rate of Interest	Rate of Discount											
	5		6		7		8		9		10	
	G=0	5	0	5	0	5	0	5	0	5	0	5
2	12.9	21.2	16.7	24.0	20.0	28.9	23.4	33.8	26.6	37.9	29.5	41.8
3	8.6	14.1	12.5	18.0	16.0	23.2	19.5	28.2	22.8	32.5	25.8	36.6
4	4.3	7.1	8.3	12.0	12.0	17.4	15.6	22.5	19.0	27.0	22.1	31.4
5	0	—	4.2	6.0	8.0	11.5	11.7	16.9	15.2	21.6	18.4	26.1
6	—	—	0	—	4.0	5.8	7.8	11.3	11.4	16.2	14.7	20.9
7	—	—	—	—	0	—	3.9	5.6	7.6	10.8	11.1	15.7

Table 2. GRANT ELEMENT IN LOANS OF 20 YEARS MATURITY

Rate of Interest	Rate of Discount																	
	5			6			7			8			9			10		
	G=0	5	10	0	5	10	0	5	10	0	5	10	0	5	10	0	5	10
2	22.1	27.1	31.3	27.8	34.0	39.0	32.8	40.1	45.7	37.6	45.6	51.7	41.7	50.5	57.0	45.5	54.9	61.4
3	14.7	18.1	20.9	20.8	25.5	29.2	26.3	32.2	36.6	31.3	38.1	43.1	35.8	43.2	48.8	39.8	48.0	53.7
4	7.4	9.0	10.4	13.9	17.0	19.4	19.8	24.2	27.5	25.0	30.5	34.5	29.8	36.0	40.5	34.1	41.1	46.0
5	0	0	0	6.9	8.5	9.7	13.1	16.2	18.3	18.6	22.9	25.9	23.8	28.9	32.5	28.4	34.2	38.4
6	—	—	—	0	0	—	6.6	8.1	9.2	12.5	15.5	17.2	17.9	21.6	24.3	22.7	27.4	30.7
7	—	—	—	—	—	—	0	0	—	6.3	7.6	8.6	11.9	14.4	16.2	17.1	21.6	23.0

TABLE 3. GRANT ELEMENT IN LOANS OF 30 YEARS MATURITY

RATE OF INTEREST	RATE OF DISCOUNT																	
	5			6			7			8			9			10		
	G=0	5	10	0	5	10	0	5	10	0	5	10	0	5	10	0	5	10
2	28.9	34.0	37.0	35.7	40.6	45.4	41.5	47.5	52.4	46.6	53.3	58.0	51.0	57.1	63.0	54.7	62.3	67.3
3	19.3	22.6	24.6	26.8	30.5	34.9	33.2	38.1	42.0	38.8	44.5	48.3	43.7	49.0	54.0	47.8	54.5	58.9
4	9.6	11.3	12.3	17.8	20.3	22.8	24.9	28.6	31.5	31.1	35.5	38.7	36.4	40.8	45.0	41.0	46.7	50.5
5	0	—	—	8.9	10.2	11.3	16.6	19.0	20.9	23.3	26.6	29.0	29.2	32.7	36.0	34.2	38.9	42.0
6				0	—		8.4	9.6	10.6	15.5	17.8	19.4	21.8	24.5	27.0	27.4	31.1	33.6
7							0			7.8	8.9	9.7	14.5	16.3	17.8	20.5	23.3	25.2

TABLE 4. GRANT ELEMENT IN LOANS OF 40 YEARS MATURITY

RATE OF INTEREST	RATE OF DISCOUNT																	
	5			6			7			8			9			10		
	G=0	5	10	0	5	10	0	5	10	0	5	10	0	5	10	0	5	10
2	34.2	38.0	41.2	41.5	46.2	49.4	47.5	52.7	56.6	52.5	58.0	62.2	56.9	62.8	66.8	60.5	66.6	73.0
3	22.8	25.4	27.4	31.1	34.6	37.0	38.0	42.2	45.4	43.9	48.5	51.9	48.7	53.7	57.3	52.9	58.2	63.8
4	11.4	12.7	13.7	20.7	23.0	24.6	28.6	31.7	34.1	35.0	38.8	41.5	40.5	44.8	47.5	45.3	50.0	54.6
5	0	—	—	10.4	11.5	12.6	19.0	21.0	22.6	26.3	29.1	31.1	32.5	35.8	38.2	37.7	41.6	45.5
6				0			9.6	10.6	11.4	17.5	19.4	20.7	24.3	26.8	28.6	30.1	33.3	36.4
7							0			8.8	9.7	10.4	16.2	17.9	19.1	22.6	25.0	27.3

BIBLIOGRAPHY

The following bibliography does not attempt to cover the enormous literature on general development problems and under-developed countries. It is limited to items that deal with the problem of foreign aid, and even in that field it is rigorously selective.

ABLY, P. S. J. "Beweegredenen tot Westerse hulpverlening aan onderontwikkelde gebieden." *Economisch-Statistische Berichten.* 47ᵉ Jaargang, No. 2350, 15 August, 1962, pp. 773-775.

ALTHEIM, Franz. *Entwicklungshilfe im Altertum. Die grossen Reiche und ihre Nachbarn.* Rowohlt, Hamburg. 1962.

American Assembly, The. *International Stability and Progress.* Graduate School of Business, Columbia University, New York, N.Y. June, 1957.

ANDERSEN, P. Nyboe. "Denmark's Aid to the Developing Countries",*Danish Foreign Office Journal,* No. 49. June, 1964.

ARNOLD, H. J. P. *Aid for Developing Countries.* The Bodley Head, London. 1962.

ASHER, Robert E. *Grants, Loans and Local Currencies.* The Brookings Institution, Washington D.C. 1961.

ASHER, Robert E. *How to Succeed in Foreign Aid Without Really Trying.* The Brookings Institution, Washington D.C. 1964.

ASHER, Robert E. *Multilateral Versus Bilateral Aid: An Old Controversy Revisited.* The Brookings Institution, Washington D.C. 1963.

AUBREY, Henry G. "Sino-Soviet Aid to South and South-East Asia", *World Politics,* Vol. XII, No. 1. October, 1959.

AUBREY, Henry G. *Coexistence: Economic Challenge and Response.* National Planning Association, Washington D.C. 1961.

AVRAMOVIC, Dragoslav and GULHATI, Ravi. *Debt Servicing Problems of Low-Income Countries, 1956-1958.* The Johns Hopkins Press, Baltimore. 1960.

AVRAMOVIC, Dragoslav (et al.) *Economic Growth and External Debt.* The Johns Hopkins Press, Baltimore. 1964.

BALASSA, Bela A. "The Capital Needs of the Developing Countries." *Kyklos,* Vol. XVII, Fasc. 2. 1964. pp. 197-205.

BALASSA, Bela A. *Trade Prospects for Developing Countries.* The Economic Growth Center, Yale University. Richard D. Irwin, Inc., Illinois. 1964.

BALOGH, T. and STREETEN, P. P. "Domestic Versus Foreign Investment, A Theoretical Approach." *Bulletin of the Oxford University Institute of Economics and Statistics,* Vol. 22, No. 3. August, 1960.

BALOGH, T. "Notes on the Conference" (UNCTAD), *Bulletin of the Oxford University Institute of Economics and Statistics,* Vol. 26, No. 1. February, 1964.

BANDERA, V. N. "Tied Loans and International Payments Problems", *Oxford Economic Papers,* Vol. XVII, July, 1965. pp. 299-308.

BANFIELD, Edward C. *American Foreign Aid Doctrines*. American Enterprise Institute for Public Policy Research. January, 1963.

BARKER, Dudley. *British Aid to Developing Nations*. Her Majesty's Stationery Office. 1964.

BASCH, Antonin. *The Future of Foreign Lending for Development*. Center for Research on Economic Development, University of Michigan, Ann Arbor, Michigan. March, 1962.

BENHAM, Frederic. *Economic Aid to Underdeveloped Countries*. Royal Institute of International Affairs, Oxford University Press, London. 1961.

BERLINER, Joseph S. *Soviet Economic Aid: The New Aid and Trade Policy in Underdeveloped Countries*. New York, 1958.

BERRILL, Kenneth. "Foreign Capital and Take-off" in W. W. Rostow (ed.) *The Economics of Take-off into Substained Growth*. London, 1963.

BILLERBECK, Klaus. *Die Auslandshilfe des Ostblocks für die Entwicklungsländer*. Verlag Weltarchiv G.m.b.H., Hamburg. 1960.

BILLERBECK, Klaus. *Reform der Entwicklungshilfe auf der basis bisheriger Erfahrungen*. Verlag Weltarchiv G.m.b.H., Hamburg. 1961.

BLACK, Eugene R. *The Diplomacy of Economic Development*. Harvard University Press, Cambridge, Massachusetts. 1960.

BLAU, Gerda. *Commodity Export Earnings and Economic Growth*. Royal Institute of International Affairs, London. 1963. (Roneo).

BOETTCHER, Erik (ed.). *Entwicklungstheorie und Entwicklungspolitik*. J. C. B. Mohr (Paul Siebeck), Tübingen. 1964.

BONNEFOUS, Edouard. *Les Milliards qui s'envolent*. Fayard, Paris. 1963.

BOS, H. C. "Internationale Economische Hulpverlening aan Minder Ontwikkelde Gebieden." *Internationale Spectator*, Jaargang XIV, 22 April and 22 June, 1960.

BOWLES, Chester. "Why Foreign Aid." *The Department of State Bulletin*. May 20, 1963.

BRECHER, Irving. "Canada's Foreign Economic Aid." *The Canadian Banker,* Vol. 69, No. 4, 1962.

BROOKINGS INSTITUTION, THE. *Development of Emerging Countries: An Agenda for Research*. Washington D.C. 1962.

BRZEZINSKI, Z. "The Politics of Underdevelopment." *World Politics*. October, 1956.

CAIRNCROSS, A. K. *Home and Foreign Investment, 1870-1913*. Cambridge. 1953.

CAIRNCROSS, A. K. *Factors in Economic Development*. George Allen & Unwin, London. 1962.

CAMERON, Rondo E. *France and the Economic Development of Europe, 1800-1914*. Princeton. 1961.

CARTIER, Raymond. "Attention, La France dilapide son argent." *Paris Match,* 29-2-64 (No. 777); 7-3-64 (No. 778); 14-3-64 (No. 779).

CHENERY, Hollis B. and BRUNO, Michael. "Development Alternatives in an Open Economy." *The Economic Journal,* Vol. LXXII, No. 285. March, 1962.

CHENERY, Hollis B. "Foreign Assistance and Economic Development." Paper presented to the Econometric Society, Boston. 1963. (Roneo)

CLARK, William (et al.). *War on Want* (Conference on the United Nations Development Decade). Pergamon, London. 1962.

CLEVELAND, Harlan. "The Convalescence of Foreign Aid." *American Economic Review,* Vol. XLIX, No. 2 (Proceedings of the Annual Meeting). May, 1959. p. 216.

COFFIN, Frank M. *Witness for Aid*. Houghton Mifflin Company, Boston. 1964.

CONDLIFFE, J. B. "Foreign Aid Re-Examined." *Stanford Research Institute Journal,* Vol. 7, No. 1, Stanford Research Institute, Menlo Park, California. 1963.

Council on World Tensions. *Restless Nations. A Study of World Tensions and Development*. George Allen & Unwin Ltd., London. 1962.

CURTI, Merle and BIRR, Kendall. *Prelude to Point Four*. Madison, Wis. 1954.

DANCKWORTT, Dieter. *Zur Psychologie der Deutschen Entwicklungshilfe.* Verlag August Lutzeyer, Baden-Baden, Bonn. 1962.

DOMAR, Evsey D. "The Effect of Foreign Investment on the Balance of Payments." *American Economic Review,* Vol. XL. December, 1950.

DURAND-REVILLE, Luc. *L'Assistance de la France aux Pays insuffisamment développés.* Editions M.-Th. Génin, Paris. 1961.

DUROSELLE, Jean-Baptiste, et MEYRIAT, Jean. *Politiques Nationales Envers les Jeunes Etats.* Centre d'Etude des Relations Internationales. Cahiers de la Fondation Nationale des Sciences Politiques, Relations Internationales. 131. Librairie Armand Colin, Paris. 1964.

FEI, John C. H. and PAAUW, Douglas S. *Foreign Assistance and Self-help: A Reappraisal of Development Finance.* Center for Development Planning, National Planning Association, Washington D.C. December, 1963. (Reneo).

FEIS, Herbert. *Foreign Aid and Foreign Policy.* St. Martin's Press, New York. 1964.

Forschungsstelle der Friedrich-Ebert-Stiftung. *Le Bloc Soviétique et les Pays en Voie de Développement.* Verlag für Literatur und Zeitgeschehen, Hannover. 1962.

France — Ministère de la Coopération. *Cinq Ans de Fonds d'Aide et de Coopération.* 1959-1964.

France — Ministère de la Coopération. *10 Réponses sur l'Afrique. Opinions sur la Coopération entre l'Afrique et la France.* Paris. 1963.

France — Ministère d'Etat. *La Politique de Coopération avec les Pays en Voie de Développement.* (Rapport et Annexes) By Jean-Marcel Jeanneney. La Documentation française. Editions du Secrétariat Général du Gouvernement. 1963.

France — Sénat. *L'Aide de la France aux Pays en Voie de Développement.* Commission des Finances. Communication du Rapporteur Général à la Commission des Finances, No. 27. 27 May, 1964.

FRIEDMAN, Milton. "Foreign Economic Aid: Means and Objectives." *The Yale Review.* Summer, 1958.

FRIEDMANN, W. "Methods and Policies of Principal Donor Countries in Public International Development Financing — A Preliminary Appraisal." (Public International Development Financing — A Research Project of The Columbia University School of Law. Report No. 2). The Trustees of Columbia University, New York. July, 1962.

GALBRAITH, John Kenneth. "A Positive Approach to Foreign Aid." *Foreign Affairs,* Vol. 39, No. 3. 1961.

GALBRAITH, John Kenneth. *Economic Development in Perspective.* Harvard University Press, Cambridge, Massachusetts. 1962.

Gallup International. *L'Opinion publique et l'Europe des Six.* IFOP, Paris. 1962.

General Agreement on Tariffs and Trade. *International Trade 1961.* Geneva, 1962.

General Confederation of Italian Industries. *Public Financial Aid to Developing Countries.* Rome. April, 1961.

GOLDWIN, Robert A. (ed.) *Why Foreign Aid? Two Messages by President Kennedy and Essays.* Rand McNally Public Affairs Series. Rand McNally & Company, Chicago. 1962.

GUTH, Wilfried. *Capital Exports to Less Developed Countries.* D. Reidel Publishing Company, Dordrecht, Holland. 1963.

Handbuch der Entwicklungshilfe. (Six-volume loose-leaf publication.) Verlag August Lutzeyer, Köln.

HANSON, Simon G. "The Alliance for Progress: The Second Year." *Inter-American Economic Affairs,* Vol. 17, No. 3, Winter, 1963. Washington D.C.

HARBERGER, Arnold C. "The Interest Rate in Cost-Benefit Analysis" in *Federal Expenditure Policy for Economic Growth and Stability.* Washington. 1957.

HAUTMANN, Kurt. *Grundlagen und Ziele der Entwicklungshilfe.* Verlag Neue Wirtschafts-Briefe, Herne-Berlin. 1962.

HEINEMANN, Hans-Joachim. "Entwicklungshilfe, technischer Fortschritt und Terms of Trade." *Zeitschrift für Nationalökonomie,* Issue 1-2. 1963.

HEINEMANN, Hans-Joachim. "Wirtschaftliches Wachstum und Entwicklungshilfe — dargestellt an einem Harrod-Domar-Modell." *Zeitschrift für Nationalökonomie,* Issue 3-4. 1963.

HESSE, Kurt. *Entwicklungsländer und Entwicklungshilfen an der Wende des Kolonialzeitalters.* Duncker & Humblot, Berlin. 1962.

HIRSCHMAN, A.O. "Stability of Neutralism : A Geometrical Note." *The American Economic Review,* Vol. LIV, No. 2. March, 1964.

HOBSON, C. K. *The Sxport of Capital.* Constable and Company, Ltd., London. 1914.

HOFFMAN, Paul G. *World Without Want.* Harper & Row, New York. 1962.

IMLAH, Albert H. *Economic Elements in the Pax Britannica.* Cambridge, Mass. 1958.

Institut Royal des Relations Internationales. *La Belgique et l'Aide Economique aux Pays Sous-développés.* Bruxelles. 1959.

Instituut voor Sociaal-Economische Studie van Minder-Ontwikkelde Gebieden (ISMOG). "Ontwikkelingshulp der Nederlandse Overheid." *Economisch-Statistische Berichten.* 49e Jaargang, 20-10-64: pp. 982-984, 11-11-64: pp. 1030-1033.

International Bank for Reconstruction and Development. *18th Annual Report, 1962-1963.* Washington D.C. 1963.

International Bank for Reconstruction and Development. *Economic Growth, Foreign Capital and Debt Servicing Problems of the Developing Countries.* (Roneo) December, 1963.

International Monetary Fund. *Annual Report of the Executive Directors for the Fiscal Year Ended April 30.* Washington D.C. 1963.

International Monetary Fund. *Annual Report of the Executive Directors for the Fiscal Year Ended April 30.* Washington D.C. 1963.

ISLAM, Nurul. *Foreign Capital and Economic Development: Japan, India and Canada — Studies in Some Aspects of Absorption of Foreign Capital.* Charles E. Tuttle Co., Rutland, Vermont. 1960.

KELLER, Hans, "Schweizerische Hilfe an Entwicklungsländer." *International Associations.* January, 1963.

KENNAN, George. *American Diplomacy, 1900-1950.* Mentor Books, New York. 1952.

KINDLEBERGER, Charles P. *Economic Development.* McGraw-Hill Book Company, Inc., U.S.A. 1958.

KIRSCHEN, E. S. "Objectifs et Détermination de l'Aide aux Pays Sous-développés." *Cahiers Economiques de Bruxelles,* No. 24, 4e trimestre 1964.

KLATT, Werner. "Development Aid for Development's Sake" in *Soviet Planning, Essays in Honour of Naum Jasny,* ed. Jane Degras. Blackwell, Oxford. 1964.

KRAVIS, Irving B. and DAVENPORT, Michael W. S. "The Political Arithmetic of International Burden-Sharing." *The Journal of Political Economy,* Vol. LXXI, No. 4, August, 1963.

KRETZSCHMAR, W. W. *Auslandshilfe als Mittel der Aussenwirtschafts- und Aussenpolitik. Eine Studie über die amerikanische Auslandshilfe von 1945-1956 unter Berücksichtigung sowohl wirtschaftlicher als auch praktischpolitischer Aspekte.* München. 1964.

KRISTOL, I. "The Ideology of Foreign Aid." *Yale Review,* Vol. 46, No. 4. June, 1957.

KRUTILLA, John V. and ECKSTEIN, Otto. *Multiple Purpose River Development : Studies in Applied Economic Analysis.* Johns Hopkins Press, Baltimore. 1959.

LISKA, George. *The New Statecraft.* University of Chicago Press, Chicago. 1960.

LITTLE, I. M. D. *Aid to Africa.* Overseas Development Institute, London. 1964.

MacDougall, G. D. A. "The Benefits and Costs of Private Investment from Abroad: A Theoretical Approach." *Bulletin of the Oxford University Institute of Economics and Statistics,* Vol. 22, No. 3. August, 1960.

Mason, Edward S. *Promoting Economic Development: The United States and Asia.* Claremont. 1955.

Mason, Edward S. *Foreign Aid and Foreign Policy.* Harper & Row, New York. 1964.

McKinnon, P. I. "Foreign Exchange Constraints in Economic Development and Efficient Aid Allocation." *The Economic Journal.* June, 1964.

Mikesell, Raymond F. *U.S. Private and Government Investment Abroad.* Oregon. 1962.

Millikan, Max F. and Blackmer, D. L. M. (eds.) *The Emerging Nations.* Little, Brown and Co., Boston. 1961.

Millikan, Max F. and Rostow, W. W. *A Proposal, Key to an Effective Foreign Policy.* Harper & Brothers, New York. 1957.

Montgomery, John D. *The Politics of Foreign Aid. American Experience in Southeast Asia.* Frederick A. Praeger, New York. 1962.

Morgenthau, Hans. (University of Chicago) "A Political Theory of Foreign Aid." *The American Political Science Review.* June, 1962. pp. 301-309. (Reprinted as Ch. 28 of *Politics in the 20th Century* — Chicago, 1962.)

Morley, Lorna and Morley, Felix. *The Patchwork History of Foreign Aid.* American Enterprise Association, Washington D.C. April, 1961.

Moussa, Pierre. *The Underprivileged Nations.* London. 1962.

Mueller, Eva. "Public Attitudes Toward Fiscal Programs." *Quarterly Journal of Economics,* Vol. LXXVII, No. 2. May, 1963.

Myrdal, Gunnar. *An International Economy.* Harper & Brothers, New York. 1955.

Neale, Alan D. "The Flow of Resources from Rich to Poor." *Occasional Papers in International Affairs,* No. 2. Harvard University, Center for International Affairs. November, 1961.

Netherlands Economic Institute. *A Common European Policy vis-à-vis Underdeveloped Countries.* Rotterdam. March, 1959. (Roneo).

The Netherlands — Minister of Foreign Affairs. "Nota betreffende de hülp aan minder ontwikkelde landen." *Wereld-in-formatie.* 4ᵉ Jaargang, No. 3. 1962.

Nurske, Ragnar. *Equilibrium and Growth in the World Economy.* Harvard University Press, Cambridge, Mass. 1961.

Organisation for Economic Cooperation and Development. *Development Assistance Efforts and Policies in 1961. Report by James W. Riddleberger, Chairman of the Development Assistance Committee on the Annual Review.* Paris. September, 1962.

Organisation for Economic Cooperation and Development. *Development Assistance Efforts and Policies, 1963 Review. Report by Willard L. Thorp, Chairman of the Development Assistance Committee.* Paris. September, 1963.

Organisation for Economic Cooperation and Development. *Development Assistance Efforts and Policies of the Members of the Development Assistance Committee, 1964 Review. Report by Willard L. Thorp, Chairman of the Development Assistance Committee.* Paris. September, 1964.

Organisation for Economic Cooperation and Development. *The Flow of Financial Resources to Countries in Course of Economic Development 1956-1959.* Paris. April, 1961.

Organisation for Economic Cooperation and Development. *The Flow of Financial Resources to Countries in Course of Economic Development in 1960.* Paris. February, 1962.

Organisation for Economic Cooperation and Development. *The Flow of Financial Resources to Developing Countries in 1961.* Paris. July, 1963.

Organisation for Economic Cooperation and Development. *The Flow of Financial Resources to Less-Developed Countries, 1956-1963.* Paris. December, 1964.

Overseas Development Institute, Ltd. *British Aid* (Contents : 1. Survey and Comments ; 2. Government Finance ; 3. Educational Assistance ; 4. Technical Skills ; 5. Colonial Development.). London. 1963.

PATEL, Surendra J. "The Economic Distance Between Nations : Its Origin, Measurement and Outlook." *Economic Journal,* Vol. LXXXIV. March, 1964.

PEARSON, Scott and SCHMIDT Wilson. "Alms for Aams." *Journal of Common Market Studies.* October, 1964.

PINCUS, John A. "The Cost of Foreign Aid." *The Review of Economics and Statistics,* Vol. XLV, No. 4. Harvard University Press, Cambridge, Mass. November, 1963.

Probleme der Entwicklungshilfe. Schriftenreihe der Friedrich-Ebert-Stiftung. Verlag für Literatur und Zeitgeschehen G.m.b.H., Hannover. 1963.

RANIS, Gustav. "Trade, Aid and What ?" *Kyklos,* Vol. XVII, Fasc. 2. 1964.

RAO, V.K.R.V., and NARAIN, Dharm. *Foreign Aid and India's Economic Development.* London. 1963.

REDDAWAY, W.B. *The Development of the Indian Economy.* London. 1962.

RIMALOV, V. *Economic Co-operation Between the U.S.S.R. and Underdeveloped Countries.* Blackwell, Oxford. 1964.

ROSENSTEIN-RODAN, P.N. "International Aid for Underdeveloped Countries." *The Review of Economics and Statistics,* Vol. XLIII, No. 2. May, 1961.

ROSS, Anthony Clunies, with DOWNING, R.I. and others. *One Per Cent. The Case for Greater Australian Foreign Aid.* Melbourne University Press. 1963.

SALANT, Walter S. (et al.). *The United States Balance of Payments in 1968.* The Brookings Institution, Washington D.C. 1963.

SAUVY, Alfred (ed.). *Le "Tiers-Monde", Sous-développement et développement.* Presses Universitaires de France. 1961.

SCHEEL, W. "Verfahren und Formen für Zusammenarbeit mit den Entwicklungsländern", Bonn, 1961. In *Entwicklungsländer und Entwicklungshilfen,* ed. Kurt Hesse, Duncker & Humblot, Berlin. 1962.

SCHELLING, Thomas C. *International Economics.* Allyn & Bacon, Inc., Rockleigh, New Jersey, U.S.A. 1958.

SCHELLING, Thomas C. *The Strategy of Conflict.* Harvard University Press, Cambridge, Mass. 1960.

SCHMIDT, Wilson. "Default on International Public Debts." *The National Banking Review.* March, 1965.

SCHMIDT, Wilson. "The Economics of Charity : Loans vs. Grants." *The Journal of Political Economy.* August, 1964.

SCHMITT, Matthias. *Die Historischen Grundlagen der Entwicklungspolitik.* Kieler Vorträge, Kiel. 1963.

SHONFIELD, Andrew. *The Attack on World Poverty.* Random House, New York. 1960.

SIEGERT, Robert (ed.). *Entwicklungshilfe — Einmal Anders.* Verlag August Lutzeyer, Baden-Baden. Bonn. 1963.

SIMONET, Henri. *La Formation du Capital dans les Pays sous-développés et l'assistance financière étrangère.* Université Libre de Bruxelles. 1959.

SINGER, H.W. "International Aid for Economic Development : Problems and Tendencies." *International Development Review,* Vol. VI, No. 1. March, 1964.

SOLOW, Robert. *Capital Theory and the Rate of Interest.* Amsterdam. 1963.

STANFORD RESEARCH INSTITUTE. *Significant Issues in Economic Aid to Newly Developing Countries.* California, U.S.A. January, 1960.

STREETEN, Paul. "Hilfe, Handel und Entwicklung." *Schmollers Jahrbuch für Gesetzgebung, Verwaltung und Volkswirtschaft.* Duncker & Humblot, Berlin. 1964.

Swann, D. and McLachlan, D.L. "Programming and Competition in the European Communities." *Economic Journal*, Vol. LXXIV. March, 1964.

Sweden — Ministry of Finance, in collaboration with the Ministry for Foreign Affairs. *Swedish Development Assistance. A Summary of the Development Assistance Bill, 1962*. Stockholm. 1962.

Sweden — Ministry of Foreign Affairs. *Aspekter på utvecklingsbiståndet*. Promemorior overlämnade till beredningen för internationella biståndsfrågor. Stockholm. 1962.

Sweden — Ministry of Foreign Affairs. *Kommersielt och handelspolitiskt utvecklingsbistånd*. Rapport avgiven av en arbetsgrupp inom beredningen för internationella biståndsfrågor. Stockholm. 1963.

Thorp, W. L. *Trade, Aid or What?* The Johns Hopkins Press, Baltimore. 1954.

Tinbergen, J. and The Documentation Centre of the Action Committee for the United States of Europe. *The European Community and the Underdeveloped Countries*. May, 1959. (Roneo).

Tinbergen, J. *Shaping the World Economy, Suggestions for an International Economic Policy*. A Twentieth Century Fund Study, New York. 1962.

Toynbee, A. J. *The World and the West*. B.B.C. Reith Lectures, 1952. Oxford University Press, London - New York - Toronto. 1953.

United Kingdom — H.M. Treasury. *Aid to Developing Countries*. H.M. Stationery Office, London. Cmnd. 2147. September, 1963.

United Nations. *The Promotion of the International Flow of Private Capital. Progress Report by the Secretary-General*. New York. 1960.

United Nations. *International Economic Assistance to the Less Developed Countries*. New York. 1961.

United Nations. *International Flow of Long-Term Capital and Official Donations, 1951-1959*. New York. 1961.

United Nations. *The Capital Development Needs of the Less Developed Countries*. New York. 1962.

United Nations. *World Economic Survey, 1962*. New York. 1963.

United Nations. *The United Nations Development Decade: Proposals for Action*. Report to the Secretary-General. New York. 1962.

United Nations Conference on Trade and Development, Geneva. *External Assistance and the Balance of Payments of Donor Countries, Financing for an Expansion of International Trade*. Paper prepared by Professor Richard N. Cooper of Yale University — E/CONF.46/P/13. 10th March, 1964. (Roneo)

United Nations Conference on Trade and Development, Geneva. *Financing for an Expansion of International Trade*. Paper prepared by Bureau of General Economic Research and Policies of the U.N. — E/CONF.46/9. 10th March, 1964. (Roneo)

United Nations Conference on Trade and Development, Geneva. *Flow of Private Capital from Developing to Developed Countries, Financing for an Expansion of International Trade*. Paper prepared by International Monetary Fund — E/CONF. 46/20. 9th January, 1964. (Roneo)

United States. *New Program for Foreign Aid*. President Kennedy's Message to the Congress, Department of State. 22nd March, 1961.

United States. *Foreign Aid Message*. President Kennedy's Message to the Congress, Department of State. 13th March, 1962.

United States. *Report to the President on Foreign Economic Policies (Gray Report)*. Washington D.C. 1950.

United States. Agency for International Development, Department of Defense. *Proposed Mutual Defense and Development Programs (Annual), Summary Presentation to the Congress*. Washington D.C.

United States — Agency for International Development. *Reports to the Congress on the Foreign Assistance Program (Annual).* Washington D.C., U.S. Government Printing Office.

United States — Agency for International Development. *Principles of Foreign Economic Assistance.* U.S. Government Printing Office, Washington D.C. 1963.

United States — Department of Commerce. *Foreign Aid by the United States Government, 1940-1951.* U.S. Government Printing Office, Washington. 1952.

United States — Department of State. *The Scope and Distribution of United States Military and Economic Assistance Programs.* Report to the President of the United States from The Committee to Strengthen the Security of the Free World (Clay Report). 20th March, 1963.

United States — Senate, Special Committee to Study the Foreign Aid Program. *The Foreign Aid Program: Compilation of Studies and Surveys.* U.S. Government Printing Office, Washington. 1957.

United States — Senate, Special Committee to Study the Foreign Aid Program. *Foreign Aid Programs and U.S. Economy.* National Planning Association. U.S. Government Printing Office, Washington. 1957.

United States — Senate, Committee on Foreign Relations. *United States Foreign Policy: Compilation of Studies.* U.S. Government Printing Office, Washington. 1961.

United States — International Development Advisory Board, The. *Partners in Progress.* A Report to the President of the United States (Rockefeller Report). Washington D.C. 1951.

United States — International Development Advisory Board, The. *A New Emphasis on Economic Development Abroad.* A Report to the President of the United States. Washington D.C. March, 1957.

URQUIDI, Victor L. "Two Years of the Alliance for Progress." *Inter-American Economic Affairs,* Vol. 17, No. 4. Spring, 1964.

VAN DER VEEN, G. *Aiding Underdeveloped Countries through International Economic Co-operation.* N.V. W. D. Meinema, Delft. 1954.

VINER, J. "International Finance in the Post-War World." *The Journal of Political Economy,* Vol. LV, No. 106. April, 1947.

WARD Jackson, Barbara. "Foreign Aid : Strategy or Stopgap ?" *Foreign Affairs,* Vol. 41, October, 1962, pp. 90-104.

WHITE, John. *German Aid.* Overseas Development Institute, Ltd. London. 1965.

WHITE, John. *Japanese Aid.* Overseas Development Institute, Ltd. London. 1964.

WILLIAMS, Peter and MOYES, Adrian. *Not by Governments Alone — The Role of British Non-Government Organisations in the Development Decade.* Overseas Development Institute, Ltd. London. 1964.

WIT, Daniel. "A New Strategy for Foreign Economic Aid," *Orbis,* Vol. VII, No. 4. 1964.

WOLF, Jr., Charles. *Foreign Aid, Theory and Practice in Southern Asia.* Princeton University Press, Princeton. 1960.

WOLF, Jr., Charles. "Some Aspects of the 'Value' of Less Developed Countries to the United States." *World Politics,* Vol. XV. 4th July, 1963.

WOOD, C. Tyler. "Problems of Foreign Aid Viewed from the Inside." *American Economic Review,* Vol. XLIX, No. 2 (Proceedings of the Annual Meeting). May, 1959.

YANNAY, Ya'acov. *La Coopération Technique d'Israël avec l'Afrique.* Genève. 1964.

YANNAY, Ya'acov. "Technical Cooperation between Israel and the Developing World." *International Development Review,* Vol. VI, No. 3. 1964.

YOUNGER, Kenneth. "Public Opinion and British Foreign Policy." *International Affairs,* Vol. 40, No. 1. January, 1964.

FROM THE CATALOGUE

DEVELOPMENT ASSISTANCE EFFORTS AND POLICIES
1965 Review. Report by Willard L. Thorp,
Chairman of the Development Assistance Committee (September 1965)
148 pages (demy 8vo)　　　10s. 6d.　　$ 1.75　　F 7　　Sw. fr. 7　　DM 5.80

**THE FLOW FINANCIAL RESOURCES
TO LESS-DEVELOPED COUNTRIES** 1956-1963 (December 1964)
180 pages (demy 8vo)　　　15s.　　$ 2.50　　F 10　　Sw. fr. 10　　DM 8.30

**FOREIGN SKILLS AND TECHNICAL ASSISTANCE
IN ECONOMIC DEVELOPMENT,**
by Angus Maddison (November 1965)
106 pages (demy 8vo)　　　15s.　　$ 2.50　　F 10　　Sw. fr. 10　　DM 8.30

No. 1. DEVELOPMENT PLANS AND PROGRAMMES
Some case studies and experiences (September 1964)
In the « Studies in Development » series
220 pages (demy 8vo)　　　12s. 6d.　　$ 2.00　　F 8　　Sw. fr. 8　　DM 6.60

FOOD AID
Its role in economic development (April 1963)
86 pages (demy 8vo)　　　5s.　　$ 0.75　　F 3　　Sw. fr. 3　　DM 2.50

REGIONAL ECONOMIC PLANNING
Techniques of analysis for less-developed areas. Edited by Walter Isard
and John Cumberland. Bellagio Conference (July 1961)
452 pages (demy 8vo)　　　37s.6d.　　$ 6　　F 25　　Sw. fr. 25　　DM 21

**METHODS OF INDUSTRIAL DEVELOPMENT
WITH SPECIAL REFERENCE TO LESS-DEVELOPED AREAS**
Edited by Albert Winsemius and John A. Pincus. Madrid Conference (April 1962)
356 pages (demy 8vo)　　　30s.　　$ 5　　F 20　　Sw. fr. 20　　DM 16.50

GOVERNMENT FINANCE AND ECONOMIC DEVELOPMENT
Edited by Alan T. Peacock and Gerald Hauser. Athens Conference (June 1965)
316 pages (demy 8vo)　　　30s.　　$ 5　　F 20　　Sw. fr. 20　　DM 16.50

AREA ECONOMIC AND SOCIAL REDEVELOPMENT
Guidelines for programmes by L. H. Klaassen (June 1965)
116 pages (demy 8vo)　　　27s.6d.　　$ 4.50　　F 18　　Sw. fr. 18　　DM 15

**FISCAL INCENTIVES FOR PRIVATE INVESTMENT
IN DEVELOPING COUNTRIES**
Report of the OECD Fiscal Committee (July 1965)
118 pages (demy 8vo)　　　24s.　　$ 4　　F 16　　Sw. fr. 16　　DM 13.40

In the "Education and Development" Series : Country Reports
THE MEDITERRANEAN REGIONAL PROJECT
ITALY (June 1965)
218 pages (demy 8vo)　　　17s. 6d.　　$ 3　　F 12　　Sw. fr. 12　　DM 10
SPAIN (June 1965)
138 pages (demy 8vo)　　　10s. 6d.　　$ 1.75　　F 7　　Sw. fr. 7　　DM 5.80
GREECE (July 1965)
200 pages (demy 8vo)　　　12s. 6d.　　$ 2　　F 8.50　　Sw. fr. 8.50　　DM 7
YUGOSLAVIA (July 1965)
146 pages (demy 8vo)　　　17s. 6d.　　$ 3　　F 12　　Sw. fr. 12　　DM 10
TURKEY (July 1965)
192 pages (demy 8vo)　　　15s.　　$ 2.50　　F 10　　Sw. fr. 10　　DM 8.30

INVENTORY OF TRAINING POSSIBILITIES IN EUROPE (February 1965)
896 pages (demy 8vo)　　　52s. 6d.　　$ 8.50　　F 35　　Sw. fr. 35　　DM 29

OECD SALES AGENTS
DÉPOSITAIRES DES PUBLICATIONS DE L'OCDE

ARGENTINA - ARGENTINE
Editorial Sudamericana S.A.,
Alsina 500, BUENOS AIRES.

AUSTRALIA - AUSTRALIE
B.C.N. Agencies Pty, Ltd.,
62 Wellington Parade, East MELBOURNE, C.2.

AUSTRIA - AUTRICHE
Gerold & Co., Graben 31, WIEN 1.
Sub-Agent : GRAZ : Buchhandlung Jos. A. Kienreich, Sackstrasse 6.

BELGIUM - BELGIQUE
Standaard Wetenschappelijke Uitgeverij,
Belgiëlei 147, ANVERS.
Librairie des Sciences (R. Stoops),
76-78, Coudenberg. BRUXELLES.

CANADA
Queen's Printer - Imprimeur de la Reine,
OTTAWA.

DENMARK - DANEMARK
Munksgaard Boghandel, Ltd., Nörregade 6,
KOBENHAVN K.

FINLAND - FINLANDE
Akateeminen Kirjakauppa, Keskuskatu 2,
HELSINKI.

FORMOSA - FORMOSE
Books and Scientific Supplies Services, Ltd.
P.O.B. 83, TAPEI.
TAIWAN.

FRANCE
Bureau des Publications de l'OCDE,
2, rue André-Pascal, PARIS (16e).
Principaux sous-dépositaires :
PARIS : Presses Universitaires de France,
49, bd Saint-Michel, 5e
Librairie de Médicis, 3, rue de Médicis, 6e
Sciences Politiques (Lib.), 30, rue Saint-Guillaume, 7e
La Documentation Française, 16, rue Lord Byron, 8e
AIX-EN-PROVENCE : Librairie de l'Université.
BORDEAUX : Mollat.
GRENOBLE : Arthaud.
LILLE : Le Furet du Nord.
LYON 2e : L. Demortière.
STRASBOURG : Berger-Levrault.

GERMANY - ALLEMAGNE
Deutscher Bundes-Verlag G.m.b.H.
Postfach 9380, 53 BONN.
Sub-Agents : BERLIN 62 : Elwert & Meurer.
MUNCHEN : Hueber, HAMBURG : Reuter-Klöckner; und in den massgebenden Buchhandlungen Deutschlands.

GREECE - GRÈCE
Librairie Kauffmann, 28, rue du Stade, ATHÈNES-132.

ICELAND - ISLANDE
Snæbjörn Jónsson & Co., h.f., Hafnarstræti 9,
P.O. Box 1131, REYKJAVIK.

INDIA - INDE
International Book House Ltd.,
9 Ash Lane, Mahatma Gandhi Road, BOMBAY 1.
Oxford Book and Stationery Co. :
NEW DELHI, Scindia House.
CALCUTTA, 17 Park Street.

IRELAND - IRLANDE
Eason & Son, 40-41 Lower O'Connell Street,
DUBLIN.

ISRAEL
Emanuel Brown,
35 Allenby Road, and 48 Nahlath Benjamin St.,
TEL-AVIV.

ITALY - ITALIE
Libreria Commissionaria Sansoni
Via Lamarmora 45, FIRENZE.
Via Paolo Mercuri 19/B, ROMA.

Sous - Dépositaires : GENOVA : Libreria Di Stefano. MILANO : Libreria Hœpli. NAPOLI : Libreria L. Cappelli. PADOVA : Libreria Zannoni. PALERMO : Libreria C. Cicala Inguaggiato. ROMA : Libreria Rizzoli, Libreria Tombolini. TORINO Libreria Lattes.

JAPAN - JAPON
Maruzen Company Ltd.,
6 Tori-Nichome Nihonbashi, TOKYO.

KENYA
New Era Publications
Ghale House, Government Road,
P.B. 6854.
NAIROBI.

LEBANON-LIBAN
Redico
Immeuble Edison, Rue Bliss, B.P. 5641,
BEYROUTH.

LUXEMBOURG
Librairie Paul Bruck
22, Grand' Rue,
LUXEMBOURG.

MALTA - MALTE
Labour Book Shop, Workers' Memorial Building,
Old Bakery Street, VALLETTA.

MOROCCO - MAROC
Éditions La Porte, Aux Belles Images.
281, avenue Mohammed V, RABAT.

THE NETHERLANDS - PAYS-BAS
W.P. Van Stockum & Zoon,
Buitenhof 36, DEN HAAG.

NEW ZEALAND - NOUVELLE ZÉLANDE
Government Printing Office,
20 Molesworth Street (Private Bag), WELLINGTON
and Government Bookshops at
Auckland (P.O.B. 5344)
Christchurch (P.O.B. 1721)
Dunedin (P.O.B. 1104).

NORWAY - NORVÈGE
A/S Bokhjornet, Lille Grensen 7, OSLO.

PAKISTAN
Mirza Book Agency, 65, The Mall, LAHORE 3

PORTUGAL
Livraria Portugal, Rua do Carmo 70, LISBOA.

SOUTH AFRICA - AFRIQUE DU SUD
Van Schaik's Book Store Ltd.,
Church Street, PRETORIA.

SPAIN - ESPAGNE
Mundi Prensa, Castelló 37, MADRID.
Libreria Bastinos de José Bosch, Pelayo 52,
BARCELONA 1.

SWEDEN - SUÈDE
Fritzes, Kungl. Hovbokhandel,
Fredsgatan 2, STOCKHOLM 16.

SWITZERLAND - SUISSE
Librairie Payot, 6, rue Grenus, 1211 GENÈVE, 11
et à LAUSANNE, NEUCHATEL, VEVEY,
MONTREUX, BERNE, BALE et ZURICH.

TURKEY - TURQUIE
Librairie Hachette, 469 Istiklal Caddesi, Beyoglu,
ISTANBUL et 12 Ziya Gökalp Caddesi, ANKARA.

UNITED KINGDOM - ROYAUME-UNI
H.M. Stationery Office, P.O. Box 569, LONDON,
S.E.1.
Branches at : EDINBURGH, BIRMINGHAM,
BRISTOL, MANCHESTER, CARDIFF, BELFAST.

UNITED STATES OF AMERICA
OECD Publications Center, Suite 1305,
1750 Pennsylvania Ave, N. W.
WASHINGTON, D.C. 20006.

YUGOSLAVIA - YOUGOSLAVIE
Jugoslovenska Knjiga, Marsala Tita, 23, P.O.B. 36,
BEOGRAD.

Les commandes provenant de pays où l'OCDE n'a pas encore désigné de dépositaire
peuvent être adressées à :
OCDE, Bureau des Publications, 2, rue André-Pascal, Paris (16e).
Orders and inquiries from countries where sales agents have not yet been appointed may be sent to
OECD, Publications Office, 2, rue André-Pascal, Paris (16e).

OECD PUBLICATIONS
2, rue André-Pascal, Paris XVIe
No. 19,649. February 1966.

PRINTED IN BELGIUM